RANGER
North American Frontier Soldier

Matt Wulff

HERITAGE BOOKS
2008

HERITAGE BOOKS
AN IMPRINT OF HERITAGE BOOKS, INC.

Books, CDs, and more—Worldwide

For our listing of thousands of titles see our website
at
www.HeritageBooks.com

Published 2008 by
HERITAGE BOOKS, INC.
Publishing Division
100 Railroad Ave. #104
Westminster, Maryland 21157

Copyright © 2008 Matt Wulff

Other books by the author:
Robert Rogers' Rules for the Ranging Service: An Analysis

All rights reserved. No part of this book may be reproduced or transmitted in any form or by any means, electronic or mechanical, including photocopying, recording or by any information storage and retrieval system without written permission from the author, except for the inclusion of brief quotations in a review.

International Standard Book Numbers
Paperbound: 978-0-7884-4678-8
Clothbound: 978-0-7884-7197-1

Dedication

This book is dedicated to John C. Jaeger, Major and co-founder of Jaeger's Battalion of Rogers Rangers. He left our ranks on January 11th, 2008.

John, you will be truly missed.

Table of Contents

Illustrations, Maps, and Photographs..v
Acknowledgements..vii
Preface..ix

Colonization and Conflict 1
The Ranger Concept... 27
Benjamin Church's Rangers 35
New England Snowshoe Men 65
John Lovewell's Rangers.. 73
John Gorham's Rangers... 83
Joseph Gorham's Rangers 89
Robert Rogers' Rangers... 95
James Smith's Rangers 127
Sam Brady's Rangers... 137
Epilogue 147
Bibliography..149
Index..155
About the Author..163

Illustrations, Maps, and Photographs

Maps

1. Outline map of the eastern half of the present day United States of America showing the locations of 17th and 18th century French fortifications in North America. A legend of location names to match the numbered areas on the map is on the following page.

2. Outline map of the eastern half of the present day United States of America showing the locations of 17th and 18th century British fortifications in North America. A legend of location names to match the numbered areas on the map is on the following page.

Illustrations

1. Woodcut print of Captain Benjamin Church

2. 1705 drawing of the rebuilt fort at Casco Harbor.

3. Woodcut print of the Deerfield Massacre.

Photographs

1. Native American re-enactor Dan Reese out-fitted in the dress of an Indian warrior from King Philip's War, armed with a traditional hickory bow.

2. The Author and friend, Tom Shisler, dressed and equipped as Rangers scouting the frontier for any sign of the enemy.

3. The Author dressed in clothing typical of the New England Snowshoe Men, with his toboggan packed for a long scout.

4. The Author dressed in civilian clothing typical of that used by John Lovewell's Rangers. He is armed with a fowling piece and has his knapsack and blanket roll ready for the march.

5. Dan Reese is dressed and equipped as one Robert Rogers' Stockbridge Rangers.

Acknowledgments

I have many peoples to thank for all of their help during the writing of this book, which is meant to be a companion to my 1st book, "Robert Rogers Rules for the Ranging Service An Analysis," which was published by Heritage Books in April of 2006.

Tim Todish of Grand Rapids, Michigan. Tim continues to be my mentor and a good friend who is always willing to share his knowledge of the 17th and 18th centuries.

Gary Zaboly of Bronx, New York. A good friend and trusted email correspondent concerning the topic of the Rangers of the colonial period. You have never ceased to answer the many questions I have shot your way. I hope one day we may meet in person.

Thomas Pray of Peru, New York. Your knowledge of the New York area, especially the Lake George/Lake Champlain corridor has made for some fine discussions under the company fly at historical events. I hope we both continue on our search for the "Holy Grail" of the Ranging Service for many years to come.

George Bray of Rochester, New York. A fine author and historian, you are always willing to share your vast knowledge of the colonial period with me.

Tom Shisler of Sugar Grove, Ohio. You always serve as a reminder that what we do should be fun, and to not let it turn into something that feels like a chore to do. When that happens, it is time to get out of the hobby.

Tim Green of Macedon, New York. You were a big help in researching Benjamin Church. I can't thank you enough.

Jerry Knitis of Hilton, New York. Thanks for all of your help with research materials.

My parents Gary and Sharon Wulff. You both have never failed to support me, and to provide encouragement when I needed it the most.

My Son Michael and his wife Heather. It has been a real delight for me to see the two of you start your life together. It helps to remind me of what is really important in life.

My Daughter Brittany. Your determination for your work in both life and in school is a constant encouragement for me to keep trying to accomplish things in life.

And of course my dear wife Beth without whom I would be nothing. You are the best thing that has ever happened to me. I hope we have many more years together in which to continue our adventure.

Finally I would like to thank God, by whose grace and mercy I have been allowed to take this latest journey in history, meager as it may be.

Preface

This book is being written as a companion to my 1st book "Robert Rogers Rules for the Ranging Service An Analysis." It is a look at a small sampling of the various Ranger units of the 17th and 18th centuries in North America. The units discussed within these pages are some of the more famous of these early Special Forces. I have only focused on two Ranger units from the Revolutionary War period, although there were many, because the concept of the Ranger as a frontier soldier had changed somewhat during this time period. I do not mean to slight any of these units, but I am rather just trying to stick to the units that were the guardians of our frontiers. James Smith would raise a company of rangers during Pontiac's Rebellion, and then command a Battalion of riflemen during the revolution. The other Revolutionary War unit is Captain Sam Brady's Rangers. Brady's Rangers protected the frontiers of Virginia, and Pennsylvania from Indian attacks. Brady's unit, if any, truly operated as guardians of the frontier.

During the colonization of North America by world powers such as France, Great Britain, and Spain, the need for a military presence in the new world became clearly evident. Conflicts between the Native Americans and European traders and settlers were bound to happen, if for no other reason than the vast differences in the way these two groups of people existed, not to mention any spiritual or racial beliefs. In addition to conflicts with the Native Americans, conflicts over land, trading, fishing rights and a large host of others would cause open warfare between the colonists themselves.

To protect their claims and intentions in the new world the Monarchs of Great Britain and France sent regular troops to be stationed in North America, although for Britain this usually meant some military personnel to train the colonists to fight for themselves, along with some naval support. It was felt that the presence of these troops would bring about a stabilizing effect on colonial relations between the two empires, but the conflicts did not cease. It also became evident that these highly trained regular soldiers would have to adapt to a very different way of fighting in North America. European military tactics that had been developed for years, and while highly effective in Europe, were not nearly as effective in the vast forests and undeveloped frontiers of the new world, especially when your enemy would not fight on your terms.

The French forces early on adapted in a much better way to these changes than did the forces of Great Britain. New France developed a militia system utilizing French Canadian born partisans that were well equipped for fighting in North America, on all kinds of terrain, and in all sorts of inclement weather. Strong alliances with a vast number of Native American tribes who not only fought along side of the Canadian inhabitants, but taught them their methods of warfare and tactics suited for woodland fighting, intensified France's ability to wage war in North America. This became what was known as "La Petite Guerre" or "The little War," what we know today as guerila warfare. This style of warfare utilized the inhabitants of Canada in a most proficient manner. British regular troops, using linear tactics developed over years of fighting overseas, found it very hard to fight an enemy who hid behind trees and would not come out into the open and fight as proper European soldiers should do. France also established companies of what were known as "Companie Franches de la Marine." These troops combined European military tactics with those adaptations made in the new world to establish a very well trained and efficient fighting force for waging warfare in North America. These troops even incorporated weapons and items of dress used by the Canadian inhabitants and their Native American allies into their uniforms and gear to better suit this new style of fighting. Items such as Indian leggings and moccasins were much better suited for use on the frontier of New France.

Great Britain and her American colonies also established colonial militia units to help protect the King's interests along the eastern coast of North America, but in a much different way than that utilized by the French government. Militia organizations in the colonies of Great Britain were established much as they were in the old country. England for centuries had not wanted to be shouldered with the expense of keeping and maintaining a large army, instead using organized groups of citizen soldiers to defend the King's realm. Militias in New England and further south followed this basic principle, although slightly altered to reflect their needs in the new world. Early settlements established in places such as Massachusetts Bay, Connecticut, and Virginia realized the need for protection from the threat of attack by Native Americans and from that of England's rivals. These militia groups, which were supported by levies that paid for their expenses, were highly organized into companies and squads, but they still based their training on the European military tactics brought over the Atlantic with them from England. The systems of establishing these militias varied greatly between the colonies. More densely populated areas in New England used a system based upon the founding of a new town. After the town's local government was formed, each town then formed one or more militia companies soon after. Less populated areas were often organized as county wide militias, such as those on the edges of the frontier. Militias would form together under the guidance of a company Captain and his subordinate officers for training, or what was known as a "muster." These periods when a militia was mustered together for training might be held monthly, or even as low as a couple of times a year, which did not help to develop a sound system of training. Often the militia men were required to bring along their own weapons and gear as part of their military duties. The long distances some county militias had to travel to assemble for a perceived threat, coupled with what was at times inadequate training did little to stymie the raids that the French and the Native Americans undertook against the settlements along the frontier of the British colonies. An early warning system and a citizen soldier that could better wage the woodland style of warfare was desperately needed to safeguard the border settlements. With this need, the Ranger was born.

Today's modern United States Army Rangers trace their lineage back to the early Ranging units of the 17th and 18th centuries. In fact, when the Rangers established the Ranger Hall of Fame at their training center at Fort Benning, Georgia in 1992, Captain Benjamin Church and Major Robert Rogers were inducted into the inaugural class. The motto of the United States Army Rangers is "Rangers Lead the Way." This couldn't ring anymore true.

Matt Wulff
Custar, Ohio
December 30, 2007

Colonization and Conflict

Early European attempts at exploration focused on trying to find a new and shorter route to the Orient for purposes of trade, but with the discovery of North America and its vast natural resources, these attempts soon turned from the thought of exploration to that of colonization. Two of the major players in the attempt to colonize the new world were France and Great Britain.

France established colonies beginning in the 16th century in much of eastern North America. Fortifications and settlements were established at what would become Quebec and Montreal in Canada, areas along the great lakes such as Detroit, and in the south at sites that would become Baton Rouge and New Orleans. Under the reign of King Francis the 1st exploration of North America began in earnest. An extensive voyage by explorer Jacques Cartier in the early 1500's looking for a water route to the Pacific Ocean failed, but Cartier did explore much of the Atlantic coast and that of present day Canada. Later in 1534 Cartier was sent on the first of many voyages to explore the coast of Newfoundland and the regions of the St. Lawrence River. On his third exploration voyage in 1541, one of Cartier's intentions was to establish a permanent settlement along the St. Lawrence. In late summer of 1541 this was accomplished with the building of a fortified settlement at Charlesbourg-Royal, or what is now the present site of Cap-Rouge, Quebec. Cartier also established a second fortification on a cliff overlooking the original fortification for added protection. This fledgling colony struggled to survive and was abandoned after attacks by area Native Americans, disease, and harsh weather took their toll on the settlers of what was supposed to be the start of New France. Another attempt at colonization occurred in 1562 when King Charles of France ordered Jean Ribault to found a colony in North America. Ribault explored along the St. Johns River near present day Jacksonville, Florida, and then attempted a settlement at Parris Island, in what is now South Carolina, but this post also failed. The French returned to the St. Johns River area and built Fort Caroline in 1564. The Spanish were also trying to colonize North America at this time, and had established St. Augustine a little further south. The Spanish ordered out troops to attack Fort Caroline to dislodge what the Spanish felt were French interlopers into their lands. The fort was destroyed after a successful attack, and any permanent presence of the French in North America was once again thwarted.

After these initial failures France would limit their interest in North America to the vast fishing in the Grand Banks off of Newfoundland for the next several years. French interest in the new world would be renewed in the early 17th century when they tried to establish a foothold in the fur trade with the Native American tribes. In order to do this France would have to establish fur trading posts, and send traders into the interior of the continent to reach and promote better trade with a larger portion of the Native American population. In 1599 the first fur trading post was established at Tadoussac, near the mouth of the Saguenay River. Samuel de Champlain would come to North America on a fur trading expedition in 1608, which once again brought to the forefront the need to establish permanent colonies in the new world. This expedition escalated the drive to create New France. French fur posts soon emerged farther into the interior of the continent along the St. Lawrence River at "Ville Marie," (present day Montreal) and at what would become Quebec City in 1608. A centralized colony would help to support any outlying fur trade posts, and become a hub of trade in Canada. Alliances made with area Native American tribes such as the Huron and Ottawa, pledging to help them against their natural enemies the Iroquois, helped to cement the bond between France and the local tribes. Using the Great Lakes and their tributaries for travel the French fur traders had quickly moved across the continent as far as modern day Wisconsin by 1634. Actual populations around the areas in which France carried on the fur trade were rather small, but by treaties with the natives, and by discovery, France laid claim to vast stretches of North America.

In order to strengthen their foothold, and to stabilize this latest attempt at colonization, France actively recruited new inhabitants for the post at Montreal. One hundred new arrivals from France in 1653 likely saved what had become the makings of a small settlement from collapsing. If not for this influx of new settlers the post at Montreal may have been just another failure to colonize New France. By 1666 there were around 3000 French inhabitants living in French Canada. Of course this effort at colonization was still mainly to support what was turning out to be a very lucrative trade in fur, but that had all changed in 1663 when King Louis XIV decreed New France an official royal colony. This decree put more emphasis on the creation of successful colonies, not only to reap the economic bounties available in North America, but to expand the Empire of France.

The population of New France was made up of almost all men at this time, but the King made an attempt to remedy this by sending a ship with 775 women aboard to North America to become potential brides for the male inhabitants. This stratagem had the desired effect. By 1673 the population had grown to around 7000 inhabitants, 15,000 by 1689, and to the staggering number of around 85,000 by 1754.

To control the vitally important water routes by which trade and travel was made possible into the undeveloped interior of the continent, the French Government would attempt to control the Mississippi River and it environs by sending Rene' Robert Cavelier, Sieur de la Salle to explore the Mississippi River and claim it for France in 1682. La Salle named the territory "Louisiane" in honor of King Louis. The colony of Louisiana was founded in 1699. Fur trading posts and fortifications were built along the Mississippi River all the way to present day New Orleans. Fortifications along the St Lawrence River, the Great Lakes, and the Ohio River Valley combined with those on the Mississippi to secure all of these areas for France.

This line of fortifications and outposts would turn out to be a very efficient method of bringing in trade goods to the native tribes, as well as allowing the French to export furs back to Europe. Ships coming to the continent from France could link up with the French colonies in two places, the Gulf of Mexico, or at the St. Lawrence River.

The outline map on the next page also shows how this line of fortifications could be used to prevent any westward expansion of the British colonies, monopolizing their control of the fur trade. It is easy to see how the English could be trapped against the east coast of the continent.

4   Ranger: North American Frontier Soldier

This map shows the outline of the eastern half of the present day United States of America. The numbers correspond to the numbered title of a 17th or 18th century French fortification on the map legend on the following page. Numbers on locations outside of the outline of the United States are in Canada and Nova Scotia.

French Fortifications
Map Legend

1. Fortress Louisbourg
2. Fort Beausejour
3. Quebec
4. Trois Rivieres
5. Montreal
6. Fort Frontenac
7. Fort Niagara
8. Fort Chambly
9. Fort St. John
10. Fort St. Frederic
11. Fort Carillon
12. Fort Detroit
13. Fort Michilimackinac
14. Fort Presque Isle
15. Fort Le Boeuf
16. Fort Machault
17. Fort Duquesne
18. Fort de Chartres
19. Fort L' Assomption
20. Fort Roselie
21. Fort Toulouse
22. Fort Louis

This leads us to the attempts at colonizing North America by Great Britain. The British Empire was not idle by a long shot during the attempts by France to monopolize the fur trade. The lure of profit and an expanded empire fueled the drive towards colonizing North America. During the late 1500's Great Britain allowed groups of land and trade speculators, as well as people seeking relief from religious persecution, to attempt to establish colonial settlements along the eastern coast of the continent. These colonies ranged from the coast of Newfoundland to as far south as Florida. This large stretch of land was originally known as "Virginia," named after Queen Elizabeth the 1st. Early attempts met with failure much like those of the French. Roanoke Colony established at Roanoke Island on the outer banks of present day North Carolina was one such failure. This attempt at establishing a colony was organized by Sir Walter Raleigh. Founded in 1585, and supplied through 1587, a period of three years went by without further supplies or support from England. In 1590 when a relief ship with supplies finally made the voyage to the settlement, it was found mysteriously abandoned. The mystery continues to this day with the theory that the colonists were either slaughtered by the Spanish, or by the local Native Americans. Another attempt in what is now the state of Maine, the Popham Colony, was founded in 1607, but was deserted after only a year.

The first taste of success came at the Jamestown Settlement when a group of 104 men and boys began to build homes along the James River in present day Virginia in 1607. This colony was financed by the "Virginia Company of London," who expected to reward its stockholders by exporting North America's natural resources back to England, where there was a growing market for such goods as lumber and furs, to name only a couple.

Other successful colonies soon followed that of Jamestown. The Plymouth Colony was founded in 1620 by a group of refugees who wanted to turn away from the Church of England. Colonies at Massachusetts Bay, Connecticut, and Rhode Island were established by Puritans seeking religious freedom in the new world.

A new system of colonization was set up through a network of Independent Proprietary Governors to found and run the governments of some of the English colonies. People from all walks of life began to come to North America to try and find a better life for themselves, fishermen wanting to try their hand at making a living from the rich waters of the Atlantic Ocean along the eastern seaboard, farmers seeking fertile lands upon which to live independently on their own hook, and shipbuilders building and repairing the great ships that began to make the long trips back to England filled with exports from North American shores, and then returning, laden with supplies and the latest goods from Europe, all to replenish the growing colonies and their expanding populations. The Hudson's Bay Company was chartered in 1670 by a group of English stockholders in an attempt to establish a British presence in the lucrative North American fur trade. The company's charter allowed them to build fortifications and trading posts on all lands around Hudson's Bay which had waterways feeding the bay. The establishment of the company was of course in direct competition with French fur trade interests, and led to many conflicts between France and England. A few shiploads of cheaply manufactured goods from England would secure the same ship returning to England with its cargo holds overflowing with fur from North America. The populations of the English colonies literally exploded when compared to the population of New France. By 1760 there were estimated to be 1,600,000 people inhabiting the colonies of Great Britain in North America. Britain's empire and its colonies were growing by leaps and bounds as its seaboard towns became small cities.

The outline map on the following page shows the English line of fortifications built along the east coast of the continent. It is clear to see that other than Fort Loudoun, the English have been kept pretty close to the eastern seaboard in their efforts at colonization.

8   Ranger: North American Frontier Soldier

This map shows 17th and 18th century British fortifications. The numbers outside of the outlines again show locations in either Canada or Nova Scotia. The map legend on the next page lists the corresponding fortification to the numbered position of the map.

British Fortifications
Map Legend

1. Halifax
2. Port Royal
3. Fort Wm. Henry
4. Fort #4
5. Fort Dummer
6. Fort Edward
7. Fort William Henry
8. Fort Oswego
9. Fort Stanwix
10. Fort Orange, Albany
11. Fort Ligonier
12. Fort Bedford
13. Fort Cumberland
14. Fort Loudoun
15. Fort Prince George
16. Fort Augusta
17. Fort King George

Once North American began to be settled it did not take long for war upon its shores to follow. Early conflicts were between the various groups of Europeans trying to expand their profits and empires by establishing settlements in the new world. Another of these conflicts was the struggle between France and England for control of the continent during the latter part of the 1600's to the mid 1700's.

The effects of European settlement in North America were soon felt by the Native American tribes who lived here long before the first European ship came within site of its shores. Disease brought from Europe, which the native people had no resistance to, would decimate the populations of the various tribes. Smallpox could rip its way through a native village utterly wiping it out. The natives endured the loss of their homes due to the constant push for new land by the English as the population of its colonies expanded across their borders. A growing dependency on manufactured goods from French and English traders led to conflicts not only between the natives and the traders, but also between the tribes themselves as competition for fur to trade with became heated and often deadly.

The first major war fought between Native Americans and the colonists of New England was known as "King Philip's War," fought from 1675 to 1676. It is also at times called "Metacom's War," and it marked one of the first times that some native tribes would ally themselves with the English, and fight along side of them against fellow Native Americans.

The colony of Plymouth, Massachusetts owed much of its success and survival to the area Wampanoag Indians. Generally the relationship between the natives and the colonists was peaceful, but as the colonies grew, more and more towns would be built upon traditional native lands. Salem, Boston, Windsor, Massachusetts, and Providence all encroached upon the natives, pushing them away from their homes and style of living. As the towns grew, so did the tensions between the natives and the colonists. The Wampanoag, Narragansett, Mohegan, and Pequot tribes began to be viewed as enemies by the English government in Massachusetts.

Events in England were set in motion in 1660 which would change the mostly peaceful situation in New England. King Charles the II was reinstated to the throne of England, and in 1664 he declared war on the Dutch settlers of New Amsterdam, and soon captured the city. The King installed a Royal Governor there, Edmund Andros, and renamed it New

York. This served to infuriate the French in Canada who began to stir up the natives tribes in New York against the English colonists there.

Changes within the Wampanoag tribe also occurred about this same time which would further undermine the relationship between the natives and the English colonists. The Wampanoag needed access to the cheap trade goods of the English, and having them as allies helped to protect the tribe from their natural enemies the Pequot, Narragansett, and Mohegan tribes. As the need for English goods intensified, and furs by which to trade for them became more and more scarce, the Wampanoag instead began to trade their lands to the English. Massasoit, Grand Sachem of the Wampanoag, had thus always attempted to maintain an uneasy peace with the English, but upon his death in 1661, and that of his son Wamsutta under suspicious circumstances in 1662, Metacom, called King Philip by the English, became the new leader of the Wampanoag Indians. Metacom began to secretly form alliances with the other native tribes against the colonists of New England.

Religion would also play a part in the coming conflict between the natives and the colonists. The Puritans living in New England sought to integrate the Native Americans into their own society by converting them to Christianity. Several "Praying Towns" or villages where natives voluntarily sought to become Christians were soon established. These villages and the attempt to Christianize natives would also bring further tension to the region. One of these Christianized Indians would be the spark that ignited King Philip's War. John Sassamon, who after converting to the Christian religion, would become a graduate of Harvard and was able move about New England society with ease, thus he became an advisor to Metacom on relations with the colonists. Sassamon became aware of plans instituted by Metacom to attack some of the English settlements on the fringes of the frontier. Sassamon warned the Plymouth Colony officials of the plan, but Sassamon was murdered before his claims could be verified. According to an Indian witness, Sassamon was murdered by allies of Metacom because of his betrayal. Plymouth Colony investigated and arrested three of Metacom's followers for the murder, hanging them for the crime.

The Wampanoag were furious, believing that the Plymouth Colony had no right to judge and convict their tribesmen. In retaliation, several small homesteads around Swansea were attacked. Then Swansea itself was destroyed and many colonists lost their lives. The war escalated quickly with more tribes taking up the war hatchet. English settlements at Middleborough, Dartmouth, Brookfield, Mendon, Lancaster, Deerfield, and Northfield were attacked in rapid succession. In response to these attacks a confederation of New England colonies declared war on the Natives in September of 1675.

The first English response was to try and recover some of the crops that lay ready to harvest in the abandoned fields of the attacked settlements. These crops were badly needed if the New Englanders were to make it through the coming winter without starving to death. A force of around one hundred farmers and militiamen undertook the task. Not used to the tactics employed by the natives, the English force fell into an ambush, and were badly defeated at the "Battle of Bloody Brook." The attacks on isolated settlements by the native forces continued unchecked into the fall.

In early November the English forces struck back by advancing against the Narragansett villages in reprisal for the attacks on their settlements. The Narragansett's had been pretty much neutral thus far in the conflict, but the colonists began to not trust them, and so plans were made to raid and destroy their villages. The Narragansett people fled from the advance of the English army, which numbered around one thousand combined militiamen and allied Pequot and Mohican Indians. As the natives fled, they burned their villages behind them, and finally fortified themselves in a great swamp in present day Rhode Island. The English forces attacked their enemy in what would become known as the "Great Swamp Fight." The Narragansett's suffered many casualties and were forced to try and escape into the frozen swamp. The native's fortifications in the swamp were burned, including most of their stores of food stockpiled for the winter, which caused the death of many of their numbers to starvation and exposure. The English forces suffered greatly in their victory with around 70 men killed and 150 wounded. The Narragansett survivors would remain neutral no more.

Combined native forces continued to raid isolated English settlements all through the winter, even attacking the Plymouth Colony itself in the spring of 1676. The attack was unsuccessful, but it showed the ability of the Native forces to raid deep into English held territory. These raids were often gruesome with tales of torture and other unspeakable horrors becoming widespread.

The war began to favor the colonists in early 1676 as the native forces, who after surviving the winter with scant supplies, and by the loss of many of their people to sickness and battle, were unable to maintain the momentum they enjoyed early in the conflict. The English were forced to abandon some of their smaller settlements and move back towards their larger settlements and cities, but they became better prepared for native raids by fortifying these locations against potential attack. They also organized large armed groups of men to harvest and protect their crops which would ensure their survival in the coming winter. Indian raids still occurred, but did not meet with the same success as early in the war.

Aid and support from the French also never materialized as many of the natives expected. Combined forces of English and their native allies kept up constant roving patrols preventing the growing of food to sustain the Native Confederation. The Narragansett tribe was nearly wiped out in April of 1676, and Canonchet their Chief was killed. In May a large force of Massachusetts militia ambushed a party of starving Indians at a fishing camp along the Connecticut River. Over two hundred natives were killed forcing many of the bands to scatter and drift away having lost their will to fight. Amnesty was offered to any Indians who surrendered and pledged not to fight anymore.

Metacom's confederation was crumbling around him as more and more of his allies deserted him. He and his remaining followers were forced to try and hide out in a swamp near Providence, Rhode Island. Metacom was finally tracked down and killed by a Native American ally of the Plymouth Colony militia led by Captains Benjamin Church and Josiah Standish. Other than some continuing isolated raids upon frontier settlements into 1677, King Philip's war was over.

Peace would not last long, however this time the conflict began it Europe before it spilled over into North America. In Europe, King William the 3rd of England joined the League of Augsburg in war against France. This war would be known as "King William's War" in North America. It marked the first of what would be called the "French and Indian Wars" because they were fought between The English colonies, the French colonies in Canada and Acadia, and their respective Native American allies. The war started with raids against the New England settlements by French and Indians who streamed south from Canada attacking and leaving burning homesteads in their wake. The most notable of these offensive attacks by the French was the Schenectady Massacre in the colony of New York in February of 1690. A combined force of French, and Sault and Algonquin Indians left Montreal marching overland in the bitter winter weather. Arriving at the settlement at Schenectady, which boasted a strong stockade around its buildings, the French and Indian raiders found no guards posted and the settlement totally unaware of the danger that lurked nearby. The raider's original target was Fort Orange, (Albany) but when they discovered the defenseless Schenectady, they could not pass up this ripe opportunity. The bloody battle that followed was decidedly one sided with around 60 men, women and children killed on the English side, and all of the buildings and the stockade of the town burned to the ground. The French forces returned to Canada just as quickly as they came, only taking a large number of prisoners and plunder back with them.

Large scale campaigns were carried out during King William's War in North America when the English captured Port Royal, Acadia, and then launched an expedition to attack Quebec. The English failed in their attempt to take Quebec, and the French were eventually able to retake Port Royal. The Quebec campaign would be the last major battle of the war, but for the next several years, from 1693 to 1696, raids would still occur along the frontier. The Iroquois, allies to the English, suffered greatly as the English reduced themselves late in the war to fighting a defensive campaign. Without a threat of an offensive attack from the English, the French and their native allies constantly waged a war of crop destroying and village burning against their long time enemies the Iroquois. The Treaty of Ryswick in 1697 ended the war between France and England, basically reestablishing relations and borders as they existed before the war began, but hostilities still smoldered between the two empires which would not stay still for long.

The second of the four wars that would be called the French and Indian Wars began when Spain allied with France to wage war against Great Britain in Europe. This war was called the "War of Spanish Succession" in Europe, and "Queen Anne's War" in North America. This war would turn into not just one of conflict between the French and English colonists and their native allies, but to that of which empire would take control of the continent. The war would begin in 1702 and last until 1713. In 1702, the English would attack the Spanish settlement at St. Augustine, Florida, but were unable to dislodge the Spanish troops from their strong fortress there, so they abandoned the campaign. The Spanish would retain control of Florida for many years to come.

The war in the English colonies would once again be one of raids against their frontiers by French and Indian forces that traveled down from Canada, burned settlements, took prisoners and plunder in New York and the other New England colonies, and then fled back to the safety of Canada leaving the dead and dying in their wake. The settlement of Deerfield, Massachusetts would suffer a massacre of their townspeople and have their homes destroyed in 1704. Raids from Native tribes in the Ohio and Kentucky territories fell upon English settlements in South Carolina. Military aid from England did little to help these defenseless towns. Frontier militias would muster at the first sound of an alarm, but by the time they arrived on the scene of a French attack they were usually too late to do any real good but bury the dead, and provide help to those who had survived. Colonial fortifications built to protect the frontier were too widespread to stop the fast moving enemy from penetrating deep into the English territory, and ended being more of a place the settlers could go and "fort up" for safety, than a deterrent to French and Indian attacks.

While the frontier settlements were being ravaged English Regular forces would again attack and capture Port Royal, which was the capital of French held Acadia. A campaign to once again try and capture Quebec, the capital of New France, was launched from Port Royal in 1711, but the British invasion fleet sank, ending any attempt at the fortress city. In 1712 a truce would be declared between France and England, and the Treaty of Utrecht would end the war. Great Britain would gain Acadia in the treaty and rename it Nova Scotia. They also gained the Island of Newfoundland, the Island of St. Kitts in the Caribbean, and the territory surrounding Hudson's Bay. The answer to who would control North America, France or Great Britain, was still undecided.

In the 1720's the frontier settlements would suffer a short Indian uprising called "Dummer's War," or "Lovewell's War." This conflict mainly consisted of frontier raids, and was soon brought to an end, although tensions between the Indians and the English remained.

The third of the French and Indian Wars, called "King George's War" in North America, and the "War of Austrian Succession" in Europe, began in 1744 when France allied itself to Spain, who had been at war with Great Britain in the Caribbean since 1739. In 1745 a force of British colonists would undertake a campaign to capture the French Fortress of Louisbourg. The colonials would distinguish themselves as soldiers by capturing this important post situated to prevent any military forces from entering the St. Lawrence River and attacking deep into French held Canada using this water route.

The New York frontier would again suffer repeated raids and attacks by French and Indian raiders from the north. Saratoga, New York would be destroyed in November of 1745, causing a flood of settlers fleeing their homes on the New York frontier, establishing Albany as the northernmost settlement in the colony. A campaign made up of British regulars and English colonists was planned to attack Canada from New York, but it was never carried out.

Peace would be established between the empires with the Treaty of Aix-la-Chapelle, which returned Fortress Louisbourg to the French in exchange for Madras, India, which had been taken from the British by the French early in the war. All colonial borders returned to their prewar state and little occurred to change the face of the conflict in North America. Allegiances in Europe were shifting, and war could once again be seen coming on the horizon. Peace would not last long.

The last of the French and Indian Wars would be the largest of the four conflicts waged in North America. France and England both sent regiments of regular troops to the continent, as well as military supplies in a final effort to decide forever who would control the continent. The war in Europe was called "The Seven Years War," and appropriately enough, the "French and Indian War" in North America, although Native Americans would ally themselves to both the French and the British during the conflict. The war would begin in 1754, this time in the colonies, and then spill over into Europe. After King George's War both empires sought to protect their interests in the Native American fur trade, expand their territories, and increase their opportunities for profit in the new world, the fishing banks off the coast of Newfoundland, and the continent's natural resources to name just two.

Religion would also play a part in the effort to control the continent, France, predominantly Catholic, was directly at odds with the Protestant faith of most British subjects. The Roman Catholic Church in Europe held a strong influence upon the government of New France, and many English settlers, who had come to North America to pursue religious freedom, feared that if France gained control of North America, these freedoms would be lost. France also feared the same, only in reverse, and with good reason as French Catholics had long been persecuted among English territories in Europe.

France in an effort to solidify their claims of ownership of the Ohio territory, which they claimed by right of discovery, sent Pierre-Joseph Celoron in 1749 on an expedition along the Ohio River burying engraved lead plates signifying that the Ohio Country belonged to the King of France. This expedition was well manned by over 200 French Marines, (colonial troops) in order to intimidate any English leaning natives encountered along the way. This force was also charged with expelling any English traders found trading illegally on French land. The English traders would be warned to leave immediately, or suffer the consequences. The expedition was successful in placing the lead plates at various locations, many of which were promptly dug up by the ever watching natives, and shown to the English traders, who informed the English colonial governments what was going on. Otherwise the French were not well received by the natives encountered on their travels. At the village at Logstown the natives informed that they, not the King of France, owned the Ohio territory, and that they would continue to trade with whoever they wanted too, including the English who had better and cheaper trade goods. The French continued on and reached the junction of the Miami and Ohio Rivers where the large village of Pickawillany stood. The Miami Chief, called "Old Britain," was warned by Celoron not to continue trading with the English, and to return to his rightful father the King of France, but Old Britain ignored this warning. Celoron began his return to Canada not in the least bit confident that his expedition had done anything to ensure the support of the Ohio natives to the French cause.

In order to punish the Ohio natives for trading with the English, Governor Longueuil of New France sent a party to attack the village of Pickawillany. This party consisted of a combined force of French Marines, French Canadians, and Ottawa Indians. The French force successfully attacked Pickawillany, killing Old Britain and destroying the village.

To further cement their claims to the Ohio country, France in 1753 sent an expedition of approximately 200 men under the command of Paul Marin de la Malgue to establish and garrison a series of forts designed to protect the water ways and trade routes into the Ohio territory. Marin first built Fort Presque Isle, (modern day Erie, Pennsylvania) on Lake Erie, then Hacked a road across the wilderness to the headwaters of the Riviere aux Boeuf, and built a second fort there which was named Fort Le Boeuf, (Waterford, Pennsylvania).

The Iroquois Confederacy, also known as the Six Nations in New York, who claimed the Ohio country by right of conquest, became very alarmed at the French fortifications being built in what they considered their territory. The Iroquois complained first to William Johnson, an Irish immigrant who became a powerful landowner in the Mohawk Valley of western New York, and a member of the 6 Nations because of his way of doing business with the natives in the area. Johnson in turn brought the Iroquois' grievances before Governor Clinton of the New York Colony, and other colonial officials. Although British policy was to block any attempt at expansion by the French, nothing was done about the French incursion into the Ohio country.

While Governor Clinton in New York would remain idle, the same could not be said of Governor Robert Dinwiddie of the colony of Virginia. Virginia had long laid claim to the Ohio country, and considered the building of French fortifications to protect French claims there an encroachment upon territory that was rightfully theirs. Businesses in Virginia were heavily involved in the fur trade coming out of the Ohio country and had no intentions of losing their profits to the French. Land speculators in Virginia had been greedily eying the land in Ohio with the possibility of future settlement for years. Pressure was mounting upon Governor Dinwiddie to do something. In response Dinwiddie sent a young Major in the Virginia Militia, George Washington, to deliver a message to the French commander at Fort Le Boeuf demanding that the French leave Virginia lands in 1753. The French of course declined based on their claims to the same territory. A third French fort was built at Venango further enraging the Virginians.

These actions would lead to a race between the French and the English to build a fort at the vitally important junction where the Allegheny and Monongahela Rivers met and formed the Ohio River. A fortification at this point of land, (present day Pittsburg, Pennsylvania) would control the water route down the Ohio into the Mississippi River and straight into French held territories in the south. The English would build the first fort at the forks, but a large French army would soon arrive and force the small English garrison there to surrender. The English fort was unfinished, badly built, and not in a very tenable position upon the rivers edge when the French arrived. The small garrison, badly outnumbered, capitulated and returned to Virginia. The French, after destroying the English fort, would build a strong four bastion fort of their own on the point at the junction of the three rivers. This fort was called Fort Duquesne, and solidified their foothold in the Ohio country.

Washington would be sent back in 1754 to negotiate further with the French, who still refused to leave the fortifications they had built in the Ohio country, with orders to confront the French commander at Fort Duquesne. Leading his force of Virginia colonials towards their objective, Washington's native scouts informed him that a party of French troops was encamped not too far away in a glen. This French party was on their way to warn the Virginians not to advance any further into what the French considered their land. Tensions mounted as Washington and a small party of his troops crept upon the French encampment guided by their native allies led by Tanaghrisson, Chief of the Mingo tribe. In the ensuing battle, Joseph Coulon de Jumonville, leader of the French party would be killed. This skirmish, forevermore called the "Battle of Jumonville Glen," would be considered the spark that ignited the French and Indian War. French survivors fled back to Fort Duquesne leaving Washington to ponder what he may have started.

The French, upon hearing of the attack at Jumonville Glen, on what they considered an innocent party, responded by sending a large party of troops to attack Washington's forces. Washington's native scouts warned him of the approaching French, and then promptly deserted him. Returning to a place called the "Great Meadows," Washington had his men begin construction of "Fort Necessity," a small circular stockade surrounding a shelter house in which to keep their meager supplies. A shallow entrenchment was also dug around the outside of the stockade which was barely deep enough to give the Virginians any cover from enemy fire. When the French troops arrived and began to fire upon Washington's command the folly of picking this spot for a fortification was soon evident. The woods nearby were close enough to allow the French to fire from the cover of the trees, and Fort Necessity, being built in a valley, was surrounded by higher ground which allowed the French to fire down into the English entrenchments, which had become filled with water to ankle deep from an incessant rain that began falling during the outset of the battle. Washington tried to advance upon the French troops with his Virginians formed up in European linear formation, but the French, content to keep their advantage of firing from cover, would not come out to face them. Washington and his troops were forced to retire back within their meager earthworks. The firing from the French began to take its toll, and combined with sickness that began to run rampant through the Virginians, and muskets that had become badly fouled from the rain, Washington had no other choice but to capitulate to the enemy. The English force marched back to Virginia leaving the French in strong control of the Ohio country.

Even though war would not be officially declared between France and Great Britain until 1756, England would make grand offensive plans to drive the French out of America in 1755. General Edward Braddock would be sent to North America with two regiments of British regular troops and become Commander in Chief of the military forces in America. William Shirley, Governor of Massachusetts, would lead an expedition against the French at Fort Niagara, which protected the junction of Lake Ontario and the Niagara River, and controlled travel towards Lake Erie. Sir William Johnson would be sent with a provincial force to attack the French at Fort St. Frederic on Lake Champlain, which protected this waterway leading into Canada. Robert Monckton would lead a campaign against Fort Beausejour in Acadia (Nova Scotia). Braddock himself would lead the attack against Fort Duquesne to dislodge the French from the Ohio Country. Only William Johnson and Monckton would meet with success, Johnson in defeating the French at the Battle of Lake George, and Monckton against the French in Acadia, after which he began expelling the French inhabitants there. Shirley's Niagara campaign never got much past the planning stage and stalled before making any sort of progress. Braddock would suffer the most, ultimately losing his life after being mortally wounded at the Battle of the Monongahela. The French at Fort Duquesne, watching Braddock's methodical march towards them with artillery, were afraid that they could not withstand a formal European style siege. Instead a force of French Regulars, Canadians, and Natives marched out to meet the enemy before Braddock could reach the fort. The French, though outnumbered, fought from the cover of the surrounding forest using the trees and brush for protection, while the English forces tried to fight in the open using European linear tactics. The Canadians and the Native forces were able to flank Braddock's men throwing them into confusion and turning the battle into a route. The pride of the British Army in America had been turned back in the face of the enemy. This left the western frontier open once again to French and Indian raids.

Governor Shirley would assume temporary command of His Majesty's British Forces in America until Braddock's replacement, Lord Loudoun, could arrive from England for the 1756 campaign season. Little more than planning was accomplished by Shirley, although he tried as best as he could to prepare for the upcoming campaign. When Loudoun did arrive he did little more than begin to organize the army and complain about the lack of cooperation he received from the colonial governments.

The French on the other hand took this period of inactivity on the part of the English to lay siege to, and destroy the British fortifications at Oswego, New York on the southern shore of Lake Ontario. The Marquis de Montcalm arrived in early 1756 with several regiments of French regulars to take over as Commander in Chief of his French Majesty's regular troops in North America. Montcalm would lead the successful expedition against Oswego. With the surrender of these posts France controlled all of Lake Ontario and the water routes to the Great Lakes.

1756 did not turn out to be a great year for the British cause in North America

Lord Loudoun would base his plans for the conquest of North America in 1757 upon a grand expedition to take Fortress Louisbourg, which when taken, would allow the English forces to travel the St. Lawrence River into Canada to attack Quebec. A massive fleet of British warships, plus transports for a combined army of regular and provincial troops, sailed for Nova Scotia only to find a strong French fleet blocking entry into the harbor before Louisbourg. It was felt that the French fleet was too strong to attack and defeat, so the expedition was suspended, and the British forces turned back, returning home without firing so much as a shot. Loudoun felt that the English colonies were left well protected when he sailed for Louisbourg, but the Marquis de Montcalm would prove him wrong.

Montcalm would take the opportunity of the main British thrust being directed at Louisbourg to assemble a large force of French and Indians to attack Fort William Henry, built by Sir William Johnson after the Battle of Lake George to protect the southern end of Lake George. William Henry also protected the northern end of the portage route from the Hudson River at Fort Edward overland to Lake George. Montcalm's army consisted of French regulars, Canadian partisan fighters, and one of the largest and most diverse gatherings of Native American tribes to ever be seen in North America. After a week long siege, and no relief coming, the British were forced to surrender Fort William Henry to Montcalm's army. After the French burned the fort they retreated back into Canada to await the next year's campaigns

In 1758 British fortunes in North America would change drastically. William Pitt, British Secretary of State, would literally pour massive amounts of money, troops, and military supplies into the war effort to drive France from the North American continent. Lord Loudoun was replaced by General James Abercromby as Commander in Chief due to his lack of accomplishment in the war. Campaigns would again be planned on several fronts. Generals Jeffery Amherst and James Wolfe would mount an expedition to take Fortress Louisbourg. Brigadier General John Forbes, with George Washington on his staff, would march upon Fort Duquesne, while General Abercromby would attempt to capture Fort Carillon, (Ticonderoga), and then Fort St Frederic, clearing the way for an invasion of Canada up the Lake George/Lake Champlain corridor. Amherst and Wolfe, after a daring landing and hard fought siege, would force the surrender of Louisbourg.

John Forbes, although sick and dying, would methodically hack his way through the wilderness to Fort Duquesne. The French would turn back an attack by British forces before Forbes reached the fort, but not willing to try and withstand a siege by the determined Forbes, they instead burned the fort and fled overland to Fort Detroit. Abercromby would assemble a 14,000 man army and start up Lake George towards Ticonderoga in a flotilla that would stretch for miles. Rather than bring his artillery to bear upon the enemy in a traditional siege, Abercromby instead chose a frontal assault against the French outer works up the peninsula from Fort Carillon. Though vastly outnumbered the French threw back repeated assaults against their defensive works, earthen entrenchments bristling with a dense abatis of wood and brush. Abercromby, after losing almost 2000 men dead or wounded would call off the assault, and while he still outnumbered his foe by a margin of 3 to 1, retreated back down Lake George.

One high point would occur after this disaster. Colonel John Bradstreet would beg to be allowed to attack the French at Fort Frontenac on the Northern shore of Lake Ontario. Bradstreet was successful in his attack, and after plundering the fort of a vast array of supplies, destroyed it, helping to sooth the sting of the British defeat at Fort Carillon.

Montcalm's victory at Ticonderoga was in all aspects a miracle. The French government, fighting a costly war in Europe, had withdrawn almost all aid from the war in North America. Montcalm's request for troops and military supplies for the most part went unanswered, and British ships ranged the seas to intercept the few French supply ships that were sent to America, forcing the French to begin fighting a defensive war. At Fort Carillon, Montcalm had less than 4000 men, and only about a weeks worth of food to try and stop Abercromby's army, but stop them he did, turning back any invasion of Canada for another year.

The loss of Frontenac, Fort Duquesne, and Louisbourg would begin to put a stranglehold on the French forces by cutting off their outlying forts from each other. The tide was beginning to turn in favor of the British.

1759 would find the British attempting to capitalize on their successes of 1758. Jeffery Amherst replaced Abercromby as Commander in Chief, and James Wolfe, with the way along the St. Lawrence River into Canada open after the fall of Louisbourg, was given command of an expedition to take the fortress city of Quebec. An expedition was also planned against Fort Niagara on Lake Ontario led by John Prideaux.

Amherst himself would seek to reverse the loss at Ticonderoga by assaulting Fort's Carillon and St. Frederic. This plan would tighten the noose around French Canada by cutting it off from any means of relief or supply. The scattered French outposts across the continent, also without any hope of aid or relief from Canada, would be unable to survive on their own. Wolfe's Quebec expedition would drag on for weeks as the British forces tried to entice the French to come out and meet them in battle. Once Wolfe established his artillery batteries he shelled Quebec almost continuously, causing great damage to the buildings inside the town walls. The British tried several times to land troops on the Quebec side of the river and assault the fortress, but they were always driven back. The British fleet also bombarded the fortress, but nothing worked until a small passage up the rocky cliffs to the Plains of Abraham, a level open area to the west of Quebec, was found. A daring assault up these cliffs drove away the small guard stationed there. By the time Montcalm became aware that something was up, a mass of British regulars stood in ranks three deep facing the city. Hoping to drive the enemy off before they could land more troops and artillery by which to smash open the city walls, Montcalm assembled his troops and marched out to meet Wolfe's army. Fighting in European linear formations the two armies traded volleys of musket fire until the French were forced to retreat back into Quebec. Both Montcalm and Wolfe would be mortally wounded and lose their lives in the battle. Unable to withstand a continued siege of the city, the French surrendered Quebec to the British Forces.

The Niagara campaign would start off well, but a tragedy would befall its commander soon into the campaign. The British forces were able to approach Fort Niagara undiscovered after they had landed their troops and supplies and began their march on the fort. Prideaux began conducting a strict European style of siege by digging approach trenches towards the fort and establishing artillery batteries to bombard the defenders with. Prideaux was accidentally killed when he was struck by a mortar fired as he walked in front of it. Sir William Johnson, second in command, would take over as commander of the British forces. He continued to conduct the siege works as planned, moving closer and closer to Fort Niagara day by day. A French relief party tried to lift the siege, but Johnson's forces became aware of their approach and would defeat the relief party at the "Battle of La Belle Famille." Captain Pierre Pouchot in command at Fort Niagara, seeing the relief column defeated, and a section of his walls battered down by the British artillery, had no choice but surrender the fort. Lake Ontario was now completely controlled by the British.

Amherst's campaign would go very smoothly. Montcalm, before he left to lead the defense of Quebec, knowing that he did not have the men and supplies to hold out at Carillon and St. Frederic, left only small garrisons there to impede Amherst's march as much as possible. Instead of trying to hold the forts, they were to blow them up and retreat towards Canada when the British began a siege against them. Arriving before Fort Carillon, Amherst began his preparations for a siege. While directing these operations a French deserter came with the news that the garrison had fled leaving fuses lit to ignite the powder magazine and destroy the fort. Portions of the fort did blow up, but it was not totally destroyed. Amherst, instead of pursuing the retreating French, chose to rebuild the fort before moving on. While occupied with this task some of his rangers came in with the news that the French had also blown up St. Frederic and were retreating to their fortifications along the Richelieu River leading into Canada. Again, instead of pursuing the French, Amherst, after reaching the ruins of St. Frederic, would begin building a large fortification nearby which he would call "His Majesty's Fort at Crown Point." Content with the success of his campaigns, Amherst would garrison the newly built or conquered fortifications and enter winter quarters, waiting until next year to begin the final push into Canada.

In 1760, the French, trying to keep their hold on New France, would conduct their own assault on Quebec to try and win back the fortress city. Under the command of General Levis they would defeat the British at the "Battle of Sainte-Foy," but would be unable to dislodge the British from within the city walls where they had retreated after the battle. The Arrival of a British fleet in the spring forced Levis to lift his siege of the city and fall back to Montreal to await Amherst's final assault there.

The British plan of attack for 1760 was a three pronged invasion of Canada with the target being Montreal. Brigadier General Murray would advance from Quebec. General Amherst would travel to Lake Ontario, and then proceed from the west along the St. Lawrence, while the third prong of the assault would come from the south up the Lake Champlain/Lake George corridor under the command of General William Haviland, sweeping away any French resistance left in the way. The three armies converged upon Montreal, and began preparations to lay siege to the city. The Governor of New France, Rigaud de Vaudreuil, knowing that it was hopeless to try and withstand a siege, surrendered all of French Canada to the British Army on September 8th, 1760. The war in North America was over. The conflict would continue in Europe, but with the Treaty of Paris in 1763, France would cede all of Canada to Great Britain.

The British colonies would once again face an Indian war in 1763 when a confederation of native tribes would start what would be called "Pontiac's Conspiracy." This Indian confederacy, at the urging of Pontiac, an Ottawa Indian and his followers, would devise a plan to attack and capture several British fortifications at almost the same time so that the alarm could not be sent out to the other targeted forts. With great success the natives were able to initiate their plans with only Fort Pitt, built at present day Pittsburg, Pennsylvania after the fall of Fort Duquesne, and Fort Detroit, escaping capture. Unable to surprise these two garrisons, the natives laid siege to both of the fortifications. British relief forces came to the rescue of both Fort Pitt and Detroit, lifting the sieges. With these setbacks the native confederation began to fall apart, and many of the tribes would plead for peace with the British, ending this conflict.

The Native Americans, their usefulness as allies ended for now, would begin to suffer persecution to a new degree from the American colonists with their constant pushing west seeking new lands, native lands, upon which to settle.

The Revolutionary War in North America would pit Great Britain against its colonial subjects in their fight for independence from English rule. After a long a hard conflict the Americans would finally defeat the British and win their Independence. Colonization would turn to statehood as the United States of America were born.

The 18th century would end with the frontiers having had to endure war with the Native American's once again. Constant pressure to either integrate the natives into American society, or obliterate them, forced the tribes to fight for their way of life. Unable to fight the "American Dream" of expansion west, many tribes went into hiding, or simply moved west to get away from the seemingly endless flow of people coming into their traditional lands. A fragile peace would mark the end of the 18th century in North America.

Dan Reese dressed as a Native American warrior from King Philip's War, armed with a traditional hickory bow and arrows.

The Ranger Concept

The style and methods of warfare in North America would dictate the birth of a new type of soldier, that of guardians of the frontier. European military tactics, while tried and true when used against a like minded enemy, were difficult to adapt to the undeveloped frontiers of the new world. These tactics, which relied on massed units of troops, used linear formations consisting of hundreds and even thousands of soldiers. Strict military discipline was required to maintain the kind of order necessary for the success of such tactics. The movements of these large formations required large open areas in which to maneuver, and massed artillery and volley firings to force your opponent from the field of battle. Europe, which had been largely denuded of its forests in the building and maintaining of its cities, was the perfect place for such warfare.

From our earlier discussions of the conflicts in North America in the 17th and 18th centuries, one can see how it would be very difficult for a highly trained military machine such as the British Army to fight a foe that hid behind the cover of trees and cut down your men with an incessant hail of lead or arrows. The Native Americans were particularly adept at the woodland style of fighting used for years of intertribal warfare upon the continent. This was the only way of fighting they had ever known, and they became very good at it.

When the French began to settle the continent they much more easily adapted their cultures to those of the natives. French men lived among the natives and even intermarried into tribal society. A strong bond was formed between the two and the French learned much about waging war in the new world from their native brothers. French tactics, items of dress, and weapons would undergo a certain amount of change to make better use of these tactics of woodland warfare.

A common thread that becomes clearly evident when discussing the conflicts in North America between the Native, French, and British people was the use of quick hit and run raids into the English settlements by parties of French Canadian partisan fighters and their native allies. These raids would be planned against specific targets along the frontier, picked because of their isolation, and their ability to defend themselves from a surprise attack. Massacre after massacre is noted in the history of our fledgling country. Settlements such as the previously mentioned Deerfield and Schenectady would suffer greatly from these raids. The attacks were horrific in their carnage, and the many prisoners taken would often be forced to carry their own plundered goods during grueling marches back into French territory. When the prisoners reached Canada they might be sold to be used as slaves, or taken by the natives to be adopted into their tribes, or worse yet, tortured, and killed.

In order to combat this ever present threat, colonial governments and settlements would hire men to scout the frontier for any sign of an approaching enemy. This would in affect become a sort of early warning system that allowed the settlers along the frontier to seek the safety of a nearby fortification or town where the shear numbers of residents and the presence of any colonial militias might deter the enemy from trying an attack. After the threat of attack was over the settlers might return to find their homes and farmsteads burned to the ground, but at least they would be alive. The hired men would have a fixed amount of territory to cover in which they would "range" on their patrols, thus they soon became known as "Rangers." A certain type of man would be necessary to do this type of duty. Governor William Shirley of Massachusetts would require the following of Robert Rogers when he was to enlist men for the newly established "Independent Company of Rangers," Shirley ordered to be formed during the French and Indian War.

"My orders were to raise this company as soon as possible, to inlist none but such as were used to traveling and hunting, and in whose courage and fidelity I could confide: they were, moreover to be subject to military discipline, and the articles of war." (Rogers, 13)

Mainly the early rangers of the 17th century would be used in a defensive manner, but as their woodland skills increased, these men would begin to form themselves into groups who would undertake offensive missions against the enemy deep into their own territory. What better way to defend your homes than by keeping the enemy off guard by taking the war to their very doorsteps.

In the later conflicts the rangers would also adapt their methods to include that of reconnaissance of the enemy. Penetrating deep into enemy territory in order to spy upon them, and then return undetected back to their home bases safely would require the most daring of men to accomplish such a task. If possible the rangers would also utilize the skill of setting ambushes along the paths and military roads of an enemy encampment or fortification in order to possibly take a prisoner or two. These prisoners could be interrogated once they were returned into British hands for any vital information that could be gleaned from them.

Common sense and the ability to react quickly to any situation would also be a hallmark of the ranger. The weather may turn causing a scouting party to change their intended path for that of another one. A chance meeting of an enemy scout could force the rangers to abandon their mission as too risky. It truly was better to run from trouble, especially if outnumbered and behind enemy lines, and live to fight another day, than to risk an engagement you might not be able to win. The people at home were counting on you to do your job, and the rangers could not do that if they lay dead in the forest at the hands of their enemy. It was better to allow an enemy party to pass by undetected if possible and return with the information of their whereabouts and intensions. Many more lives might be saved by using your head and making calm decisions.

The rangers, in order to meet the enemy on their own terms, would have to reflect the abilities the enemy used to such great advantage when at war. They would have to be able to sustain themselves without support when operating far away from the nearest settlement, or the main army. No baggage trains would follow the rangers with ammunition, provisions, and luxuries such as tents. They would have to bring along extra ammunition and what food they could carry with them on their backs. The ability to build temporary shelters using natural materials to house themselves while on the march would be a great asset. These frontier hunters turned rangers had used this skill for years in their pursuit of game and furs.

The clothing of the rangers would often be what they arrived from home wearing. This clothing would be a mix of their civilian clothing and items of dress used by the natives to good purpose. Moccasins made of dressed deerskins were much better suited to use in the woods and swamps of the new world. Civilian or military shoes would often fall apart after only a few days of this rough use. Indian style leggings, a simple tube of coarse material such as wool or of leather, would be worn on the lower legs to protect them when traveling through the thick brush. Captain John Rutherford of the New York Independents had the following to say about the necessity of using leggings in the thick forests and underbrush.

"No man can go thro without Indian Stockings and all wounds in the Legs are Dangerous from the Climat and vermin which breed Maggots in the Wounds." (Todish/Zaboly, 297)

Coarse woolen blankets were used for cover when sleeping in the woods, but also were draped over the shoulders of the rangers "Indian fashion" as a sort of cloak. The blankets could also be fashioned into a "blanket coat" mentioned many times in journals, orderly books, and diaries of the time period.

Headgear would be whatever was brought from home and was found to be best suited for use in the woods. Large brimmed hats and tricorns became ensnarled easily in the thick brush, making them less desirable as head gear. Cut down "round hats" worked well, as did knit caps that fit close to the head. "Jockey Caps," another cut down version of a wide brimmed hat made of wool felt, were popular with the rangers as well as the "Scotch Bonnets" used by British Highland units. Even the simple handkerchief tied around a ranger's head was worn. Whatever worked well and kept the wearer protected from the various elements, wind, rain, snow, and even the sun would be acceptable.

Well made leather breeches would be virtually indestructible for the hard use a ranger's pants would see, or an "Indian Flap" or breech-cloth such as that used by the natives was worn. This was a simple length of cloth that passed between the wearer's legs and tied with a leather string or belt around the waist, leaving the ends to fold over the top of the belt and hang as flaps before and after. The use of a breech-cloth and leggings was called "Indian Walking dress" by a young George Washington who was reported to have donned this garb in order to travel more quickly on his return from his mission to deliver the order to the French at Fort le Boeuf demanding they leave the Ohio Country.

Hunting coats and other jackets of the time period worn by these men would serve their new duties as well as they did their old. References to the dress of the rangers quotes them as "wearing their clothes short," probably to make them less cumbersome than the fully skirted regimental coats of the regular army. Even though camouflage was not a term used for concealment during the early wars on the continent, the practice of utilizing clothes that would help the rangers blend in with their surroundings was in use. Earthen tones of green and brown were very useful in certain times of the year to help hide the movements of the wearer.

A great variety of weapons and firelocks, best suited for use in the woodlands, were used by the rangers. Weapons would be chosen that could be used for multiple purposes in order to cut down the amount of weight the fast moving rangers would have to carry with them. An example of this is the hatchet, which replaced the sword, as it would turn out to be a much more useful weapon and tool than a sword for use in the woods. The importance of the hatchet is further supported by this instruction by Robert Rogers to his troops in the first of his famous "Ranging Rules."

"All Rangers are to be subject to the rules and articles of war; to appear at roll-call every evening on their own parade, equipped, each with a firelock, sixty rounds of powder and ball, and a hatchet, at which time an officer from each company is to inspect the same, to see they are in order, so as to be ready on any emergency to march at a minutes warning; and before they are dismissed, the necessary guards are to be draughted, and scouts for the next day appointed." (Rogers, 55)

The firelocks used by the rangers would often be those brought with them from home, the same weapons they used to feed and defend their families with on the frontier. These weapons would most likely be common fowlers, a typical hunting weapon, or a military musket issued from the King's stores. In order to carry sixty rounds of powder and ball a method of than the standard military cartridge box, with its much smaller capacity, would have had to be used. Powder horns and shot bags, the same as used by hunters and frontier settlers, were the preferred choice. The use of a powder horn increased the chances of keeping the gunpowder contained inside dry in all of the different types of weather encountered by the rangers much better than trying to keep a fragile paper cartridge dry and intact. The use of the powder horn and shot bag in conjunction with a personal firearm made much more sense in terms of familiarity when using the weapon for battle. This is supported by this order handed down by Governor Delancey for equipping the New York Independent regiments.

"Forasmuch as a great number of men who shall enlist, or be engaged in the forces in the pay of this province, will be possessed of good arms of their own, which it is apprehended they will prefer to those furnished by the Crown, not only from their being much lighter, but as from their being accustomed to them, they will be much surer of their

Mark with those, than with Arms they never handled before;....And as a powder horn, shot bag with a case for the lock are thought more proper for the present service than the common accouterments, the Men are also to come provided therewith." - Governor James DeLancey, April 8, 1758

The scalping knife was also a weapon thought to be necessary for use by the rangers. Both the English and the French Governments paid for the scalps of their prospective enemies, making the taking of scalps a way of earning money as well as for purposes of war. It was not something that only the natives practiced doing, but both English and Frenchmen as well. The scalping knife, in many styles, was another item that would be useful for multiple purposes, including its use as a cutting tool, and that of a weapon.

The types of weather the rangers encountered would dictate the use of other types of gear just as it did when choosing how to carry one's ammunition. One of the reasons that the French and the Indians were able to carry on their war efforts so successfully was their ability to conduct raids during the most severe of winter weather. Bad weather did little to stop them from traveling into British territory, if fact, at times this would actually aid them in the fact that an attack would seem to be less likely in such weather. The weather could also help to mask the movements of the raiders as they traveled towards their targets.

The natives made extensive use of the snowshoe for winter travel, something the French would learn to use very quickly in the harsh winters of Canada. A favorite tactic of the French was to drive their enemy off of a beaten path into deep snow where they would be unable to flee their snowshoe wearing pursuers. English settlers living on the frontier would learn of the usefulness of snowshoes in their daily lives as well, and this would be a skill much used by the rangers in waging war. In fact, the use of snowshoes for travel was deemed so important that the rangers were instructed to teach the British regular troops how to use them during the French and Indian War.

The use of toboggans and sledges to haul provisions and equipment is well documented in the history of colonial France and England. Hunters had used various types of sleds to carry home their game and furs over the snow covered terrain for years. The following is a quote from the memoirs of Captain Pierre Pouchot during his years of service in the French Army about the use of Toboggans, or "Traines" by the Canadians in their war efforts.

"They also make toboggans, very practical ones to carry their equipment. They consist of two runners, made of hard but flexible wood, 10 to 12 feet long, they are used as the framework of a type of sledge, between a foot and a foot and a half in width. The base is made up of birch bark or elm wood and the front curves up in a semi-circle to pass easily over the snow. They tie their gear onto it. With straps over both their shoulders, they pull it or have it pulled by a dog. This sledge can carry 80 pounds." (Pouchot, 482)

After the "Battle on Snowshoes," when a scout of Rogers' Rangers suffered a devastating defeat at the hands of the French, some of the surviving rangers in meeting back at a rendezvous point where they had hidden their own sleds, used those sleds to help carry their wounded comrades back towards the safety of Fort William Henry.

Ice skates were another item that would be adapted for use in war. As the rivers and lakes became frozen in winter the rangers would strap on ice skates and glide up the frozen surface towards their destination mush more quickly than if they traveled overland. Forward scouts could also be sent out on skates ahead of a party marching behind them to watch for the approach of any enemy troops.

It is easy to see why the rangers are considered the forerunners of the special forces of our modern military groups. The rangers were the basis for light infantry companies beginning to be developed in the British Army during the French and Indian War. Today's United States Army Rangers carry more ammunition, and use lighter gear so they can move quickly in and out of any situation encountered. This is a lot like what their ancestors were doing over 250 years ago.

This is a photo of the Author and friend Tom Shisler, dressed as two frontier rangers on top of a large rock outcropping scouting for any sign of the enemy. Their dress and equipment is typical of that carried by rangers in the mid-18th century.

Benjamin Church's Rangers

Benjamin Church was born in Plymouth colony in 1639. Details from his early life are sketchy at best, but evidence seems to point to Benjamin being a carpenter by trade. He would become one of Josiah Winslow's, The Governor of Plymouth Colony, most trusted aids. He married in Duxbury, Massachusetts in 1667 and later would move his family to Rhode Island. From surviving correspondence one can see that Church was a very religious man, giving credit to God for the good things that happened in his life. He always felt that Divine Providence directed his very existence. Church would also hold public office later in his life from 1682 to 1684.

Church would begin work on a large farm, or "plantation" as he would call it in 1675. Plans for horses and cattle were made, land cleared, and various buildings started when the call to war came. It is of note that this man, who would become known for his prowess as an Indian fighter, was concerned about upsetting his Indian neighbors who inhabited the lands surrounding the location Church chose to establish his farm. In fact, the neighboring Sakonnet Tribe held Church in great respect, and considered him a good friend.

Church would also become a well respected military leader in the Plymouth Colony. He kept detailed memoirs of his service in King Philip's War, King William's War, and Queen Anne's War which were later published by his son Thomas. These memoirs contain specific information of the tactics his men used to combat their enemies, and are a window to the past for any historian interested in these early conflicts which would help to form our young nation. In the later conflicts he would lead missions into Maine and Canada.

This illustration is a woodcut print of Captain Benjamin Church. It is interesting to note the powder horn with shoulder strap worn by the Captain in this image. The image is public domain and used from Wikipedia, the Free Online Dictionary.

Rumors of a war against the English settlers being secretly planned by Metacom, (King Philip) Chief of the Wampanoag Indians, had been circulating for some time. The female Sachem, Awashonks, of the Sakonnet tribe sent word to Benjamin that she wished to hold a counsel with him. When he arrived at the village he found that six of King Philip's warriors were also there trying to convince the Sakonnet to join in the planned war. Church tried his best to assure Awashonks that she had nothing to fear from the English, and that she and her tribe should seek the protection of the English instead of joining King Philip in his designs against the settlers. Benjamin promised to go and seek advice about the situation from Governor Winslow, and return in just a few days with any instructions. Church would never get the chance. On his way to see Winslow he stopped at the Plymouth Colony to give warning of the impending trouble. While he was there the news arrived that the colony militia was being called up, so Benjamin reported for duty at Taunton. The natives had been stirring up trouble by pillaging houses and settlements along the frontier. So far no blood had been shed, but the militia, under the command of Major Cudworth, was ordered to march out towards the native villages to put a stop to this mischief. Church was given the command of a small party of men who were to scout ahead of the main body of troops. Church and his party, which included some "friend Indians" as he called them, moved out ahead of the army and pushed so hard towards their destination, the town of Swansea, that they were able to butcher and cook a deer they killed on their march, eating it before the main body could catch up with them. This mistake could have allowed the main body to fall into any ambush laid for them. Benjamin Church had a lot to learn about the ways of war, but there was one thing that he did discover on this march. Benjamin found out that he liked the life of a soldier. He would later write that,

"I was much spirited for that work." (Philbrick, 237)

After reaching the town of Swansea more and more militia men began to assemble there. So many men showed up that a temporary stockade was built in order to protect them from attack. A request for aid was sent out to the Massachusetts Bay Colony for reinforcements. The native forces were believed to number in the hundreds, so no moves were made until Major Cudworth felt he had enough troops to effectively engage his enemy.

The natives continued their raiding, killing horses, cattle, and other livestock on farms deserted by their inhabitants when the raids began. The Indians were careful not to injure any of the English though. King Philip had encouraged his followers that they would succeed in their plans only if the English were the first to spill human blood. It would not take long for this to occur.

A man and his son who part of the garrison at Swansea decided to go out from the protection of the stockade to have a look around the countryside. While doing so they came upon a group of Indians pillaging some of the abandoned homes nearby. The son had his musket with him, and at his Father's urging he fired at one of the natives, knocking him down. The Indian got back up, and with his companions retreated into the woods. Later that day some natives approached the garrison wanting to know why they had been fired upon, to which the soldiers responded by asking if the Indian had died, which they were told he had. The boy who had fired at the Indian was standing with the group and said that "it was of no matter" that the Indian had died. This enraged the natives. Blood had been spilled by the English first, now the killing would begin.

Within the next few days 10 people had been killed, including the father and son who had fired upon the natives. During this time many people had begun to feel that it was safe to return to their homes, or try and retrieve goods left there in their haste to flee to safety. Most were ambushed or otherwise attacked on these trips. The victims were scalped whether dead or alive.

Still the garrison at Swansea did not budge until several companies of Boston men arrived on the scene. The Plymouth men were itching to get underway. The natives had been getting very bold, approaching the stockade mocking the men inside. Two men who ventured outside to get water from a nearby well were shot and taken off as prisoners. Their horribly mutilated bodies were later found nearby.

Cudworth finally felt he had enough men to march out against the native forces. The English troops caught up with the natives, but they were separated by a river, and the decision was made to hold off an assault until the next morning. A group of 12 men, eagerly anticipating the coming action, requested permission to cross the river and attack some natives who were firing upon the English troops from the other side. Their request was granted and the men asked Benjamin to accompany them. The men, mounted on horseback, had to cross a bridge over the river, and as they did they were met with a hail of gunfire from some Indians lying in ambush on the other side. In the confusion the lead scout of the party was wounded and another man was pinned under his horse. The rest of the men fled back across the bridge to safety, but Benjamin, not wanting to leave the men behind, tried to convince the party to cross back over and rescue their comrades. Only two men would go with him, but they managed to bring back to safety the man who was pinned under his horse, and the body of the scout who had by then died from his wounds. Church after securing the men would then turn his attention to the scout's horse who was wandering away towards the natives. He was able to recover the horse, all this while enduring repeated gunfire from the enemy. God was surly with Benjamin on this day.

The action died down and the English troops prepared themselves for the next day's action. Tomorrow they would cross the bridge and assault the natives as planned. The day dawned dismal and rainy as the English troops formed for battle. Instead of being out in front again with his small company of men, Church was instead assembled on one of the flanks that supported the main body of troops. This formation was intended to push against the enemy while the flanks protected the center from attack from the side. The weather turned progressively worse causing the formation to disintegrate into confusion. Cudworth ordered his men back to the garrison house to see if the next day brought any better weather.

The next day the English troops marched to the abandoned settlement of Kikemuit which they found burned and in shambles. Marching on the troops found the dismembered remains of eight of their countrymen mounted on poles. Burying the remains, the troops continued their march to the Pokanoket Indian village, which they found deserted. The natives had fled in the face of the advancing army in great haste, leaving many goods behind, including some that witnesses said belonged to King Philip himself. Large fields of corn stood near the village which the men began to destroy in an effort to starve the natives. The Indians had crossed a nearby body of water in canoes and made good their escape. The army, instead of trying to pursue the natives and keep pressure on them, instead built what Church felt was a worthless fort on the village site.

Benjamin was still hoping to persuade some of his native friends to not join King Philip in the war, so he requested permission to travel to Pocasett in search of Awashonks. Thirty-six men and Mathew Fuller, the army's Surgeon General, would go with him, crossing on a ferry to Aquidneck Island in search of the Sakonnet Indians who had gone there for safety. The party would split into two groups, with Church's group heading south toward his farm. The party found Indian sign everywhere they looked. Working their way along the Sakonnet River they came upon two natives walking across a field of peas. Calling out that he wanted to talk to them, the natives instead started to run away from Church and his men. Chasing after them into a woodlot the men suddenly found themselves in the middle of an ambush. Church had committed one of the blunders that English troops would become known for, blindly following fleeing natives directly into a trap.

The initial volley from the natives did no great harm to Church's party, and the men began to fire back at the Indians. Exhorting his men not to fire all at once to prevent the natives from charging them while they were reloading, Church ordered his men to head for a fence bordering one side of the field. When they reached the fence Benjamin told half of his force to hide at the fence with loaded muskets, while the other half continued to flee across the field trying to lure the natives into a trap of his own. Taking a glance back at his pursuers Benjamin noticed that this was not to be the case. Instead of pursuing his men, the natives were instead trying to surround his party on both sides and trap them against the edge of the river. The only hope Benjamin's party had was to run for the cover of a stone wall that stood nearby the rivers edge, and there make a defensive stand, which they did in good order. The natives began to fire at the party behind the wall from every bit of cover they could find. Church's men were by now running low on ammunition, so he told them to slow their firing down and take careful aim when they did shoot. A sloop was seen coming towards them on the river, but as it neared the scene of battle to try and take the men aboard, the natives concentrated their fire upon it, causing the ship to retire back up the river. This encouraged the natives who continued to fire upon the defenders of the stone wall. Church and his men held out against their attackers for the rest of the day until they spotted another sloop coming towards them, this time manned by Captain Roger Goulding. Church knew the Captain, and told his men that he was, "a man for business." Sending forth a canoe from the ship all of the men in Church's party were able to get away from their attackers and board the sloop to be taken away to safety. Before they embarked, Church, the only man not yet on board, suddenly stated that he had left his hat and cutlass beside a well from which he had taken a drink during the battle. He would not leave them as a prize to the enemy. Going back into the fray he retrieved his belongings, then returned and boarded the sloop. During his ordeal

Church had one bullet graze his hair, and another just miss hitting him in the chest. Providence was again looking out for him on this day.

Benjamin Church would learn many lessons during his first campaign against the natives. He would observe the tactics used against his men, and make adjustments to the way he would do battle in the future. Many of the Plymouth Colony Militiamen who took part in the campaign were still armed with matchlock muskets and pikes for fighting in a traditional European style. It was clearly evident that these arms would not do for use in the swamps and forests in which they encountered the natives. The flintlock musket and the hatchet were much more suited for the business at hand.

The natives made great use of hit and run attacks in which they would engage their enemy, often from ambush, and then melt off into the woods or swamps before their foe could react to the initial attack. The also sought to surround their enemies, firing at them from whatever cover was available. They would not stand out in the open and trade volleys of musket fire when they could fire from a point of safety.

Church also realized that firing blindly at your attackers without aiming, in fact many early military arms did not even have any type of sights, was nothing short of a waste of ammunition. It was much better to be patient, and fire deliberately at an intended target. The natives were deadly when they could close and fight hand to hand with their enemy, using their hatchets and scalping knives with great effectiveness. Church would time and time again tell his men to keep one half of their muskets loaded and ready while the other half were reloading after discharging their firelocks, so that the enemy could not rush in on them as they could if they all discharged their firelocks at once.

Church's group was also very lucky that Captain Goulding was willing to sail into the battle and extract his men from their position at the rivers edge. Their powder and shot were almost expended when they were rescued by the sloop. If no one had come to their aid the natives could have kept up their attack until all of the English party's ammunition was spent, and then rushed in and finished them off. They must be very aware of their surroundings to not allow themselves to be trapped without an avenue of escape.

King Philip and his followers had taken many casualties during this period of fighting, and without sufficient provisions, many of those left alive started to desert him. Philip was forced to flee the area with his small band of warriors to prevent being overrun by the English troops. He successfully eluded his pursuers by entering a swamp.

The fact that King Philip was in hiding from the English forces provided no relief for the English colonies. Hundreds of natives from the various tribes had taken up the hatchet in war against the colonists. The Massachusetts Colony and the surrounding territory which included what would become parts of Connecticut and Maine were constantly under attack from raiding parties of natives. The settlements of Brookfield, Lancaster, and Deerfield were all attacked, and many settlers lost their lives. Time and time again English troops were lured into ambushes set by the natives who fired upon the English with devastating results, then melted back into the forest. The frontier itself seemed to be on fire from the smoke of the burning homes and settlements that the native forces left in their wake. Settlers by the hundreds fled their homes and arrived as refugees in the larger cities such as Boston. Food became scarce because of the many mouths to feed.

The colonies united to form an army to try and crush the native rebellion. Massachusetts, Connecticut, and Plymouth assembled their men and appointed Plymouth Governor Josiah Winslow as their General. Benjamin Church was offered an officers commission, but he turned it down. He did accept an offer to be the General's advisor, which he felt he could not pass up. The army marched out towards their intended target, the Narragansett tribe who inhabited Rhode Island. These natives had remained neutral during the early part of the war, but with all of the tensions between the natives and the colonists, an attitude that no Indians were to be trusted had begun to prevail among the English. The Army assembled and began their march, Winslow sent Benjamin on ahead to prepare for the arrival of the main body of troops at a garrison house in Narragansett country. While waiting for the General to arrive, Benjamin and a party of men went out to try and take any area natives prisoner and present them as a gift to the General when he arrived at the garrison house. The party returned with eighteen prisoners, which delighted Winslow, and added to Church's reputation as a brave man and Indian fighter.

The army, now ready for their campaign, trailed the Indians to a great swamp inside of which the Narragansett had built a large fortification by which to defend themselves from attack. A very costly battle ensued as the English troops attacked the native position. Benjamin, who was at the Generals side watching the battle, begged to be allowed to go down and fight beside his fellow soldiers, which Winslow granted, but only if Church took some troops with him. Thirty men of the reserve forces volunteered to go with him. The natives had placed a large log over a small moat at the entrance to their fort in order to try and funnel the English troops into a small area as they entered. This gave the natives inside a concentrated field of fire which greatly aided them in their defense. The bodies of the dead and dying, both English and native, were lying everywhere Benjamin looked. The English troops were finally able to force the warriors to flee into the swamp, leaving hundreds of women and children behind. Benjamin and his men followed closely, but were forced to turn back to the fort by the fire from the fleeing native forces that had begun to rally. During this part of the battle Benjamin was struck by three bullets, one severely injuring him in the thigh.

The wigwams and other buildings inside the fortress were filled with food and other supplies the natives had gathered to withstand a long siege. The English troops began to burn the fort, including the shelters which still housed the women and children. Church pleaded with the men to not burn down the fort, which along with the food found there would sustain the weakened army, which had suffered many wounded in the assault. The weather had turned very cold and the army would have to march many miles in the snow with their dead and wounded before they reached the safety of the garrison house. Wouldn't it be better to stay within the safety of the native's fort for the night, and then march back in the morning? General Winslow agreed with Benjamin at first, but some of the Massachusetts men demanded they burn the fort, the foodstuffs, and the survivors inside, even threatening to not care for Church's wounds, letting him bleed to death if he tried to interfere. Winslow consented, and the army made the long march back to the garrison house. Many of the wounded died along the way.

Benjamin slowly recuperated from his injuries until he was well enough to request permission to return home, but Governor Winslow persuaded him to stay on for another campaign against the natives in the "Nipmuck" country. Although Benjamin still had open wounds that were kept that way to drain any infection, he agreed to the request. During their march the army came upon a native village hidden in a frozen swamp. A fight ensued and a wounded native was captured when the other warriors fled the battle. After interrogating their prisoner the army continued their march, but the wounded native could not keep up, so it was decided to execute him. Just as his captor, a Mohegan Indian ally of the English, was going to strike him with his hatchet, the wounded native ran off into a swamp to try and escape. Benjamin gave chase and struggled with the Indian. Finally his Mohegan captor caught up with the two and ended the native's life with his hatchet thanking Benjamin repeatedly for not letting his prisoner escape. Continuing on their march the army had more skirmishes with the enemy, but the weather turned bad, and with their provisions nearly gone, the army returned home and disbanded. None of them were foolish enough to think they enemy had been defeated. In the coming spring the war would soon enough erupt again.

Knowing that the enemy would return, a council of war was held which Benjamin attended. It was requested that Church take command of a company of men to protect the countryside from attack. In return Benjamin offered to assemble a group of 300 men, including 150 natives allied to the English. He proposed that this force not be held inside a garrison house or fort, but to go out and lie in the woods, fighting the war as their enemies did. He had become weary and disillusioned of fighting as part of a large organized army. Benjamin was turned down because the colony was already in debt, and could not afford to finance such an army. Still not back to full health, and not having seen his wife and son for some time, Benjamin determined to return to them. Reuniting with his wife and son, who were staying with relatives because she was expecting their second child, Church returned home.

While convalescing Benjamin would not remain idle in the concerns of the war, only this time it would not be in a military fashion. He still was concerned that he was not able to prevent his friends of the Sakonnet tribe from joining King Philip in the war against the English. Benjamin began to scour the area hoping to be able to find Awashonks and see if he could convince her and her tribe to leave Philip and return to peace with the English. Church was able to help broker a peace treaty between the Plymouth colony and the Sakonnet, which in turn offered to fight with Church against King Philip. Church was finally given permission to assemble a mixed force of Englishmen and natives to fight the natives on their own terms. Benjamin received the following commission from the Governor giving him the command of the mixed party.

"Capt. Benjamin Church, you are hereby nominated, ordered, commissioned, and empowered to raise a company of volunteers of about 200 men, English and Indians; the English not exceeding the number of sixty; of which company or so many of them as you can obtain, or shall see cause at present to improve, you are to take the command and conduct , and to lead them forth now and hereafter, at such time, and unto such places within this colony, or elsewhere, within the confederate colonies, as you shall think fit, to discover, pursue, fight, surprise, destroy, or subdue our Indian enemies, or any part or parties of them that by the providence of God you may meet with, or them, or any of them, by treaty and composition to receive to mercy, if you see reason, provided they are not murderous rogues, or such as have been principle actors in those villanies. And forasmuch as your company may be uncertain, and the persons often charged, you are hereby empowered; with the advice of your company, to choose and commission a Lieutenant, and to establish Sergeants and Corporals as you see cause. And you herein improving your best judgment and discretion, and utmost ability, faithfully to serve the interest of God, his Majesty's interest, and the interest of the colony; and carefully governing your said company at home and abroad. These shall be unto you full and ample commission, warrant, and discharge. Given under the public seal, this 24th day of July, 1676. Per JOS. WINSLOW, Governor." (Church, 72, 73)

The newly commissioned Captain wasted no time in getting his company into the field. Church was to operate independently of the main army, so his plan was to range the forests and swamps looking for any sign of the enemy, and after outfitting themselves for an extended scout, the company took to the woods in search of their quarry. They began by operating in the region of Benjamin's farm, because he and the others in his group were well acquainted with the traditional paths and haunts of the natives in that area. Using this to their advantage they were very successful in capturing many of the enemy and returning them as prisoners to Plymouth colony. Using the utmost stealth as they approached their enemies, Benjamin and his men were often able to surround them and capture them all without firing a shot. Church would normally offer his prisoners good treatment if they would provide intelligence of the whereabouts of any of the other rebellious native parties, which his prisoners readily did. In fact, Church would treat his prisoners so well, especially the women and children captured, that many of the warriors in the parties would express their desire to return to the side of the English, and join Church's company and fight beside him, of which Benjamin made good use of those deemed trustworthy. Church was so successful in his endeavors that he was given leave to raise and dismiss his men as he felt needed, and to commission his own officers, which he did, even giving the rank of Captain to one of his native allies. He was also given the authority to pass judgment on his captives, able to give quarter to them or not.

Church and his men during these early days of the company established certain tactics to be used in this style of woodland warfare. Most of these were learned by watching the way his native allies operated, or by watching the actions of his enemies. Benjamin and his men would become very adept at setting ambushes along the routes being used by the enemy. Laying in concealment for days at a time the rangers seldom did they not meet with success in capturing some of the enemy. When the party was captured, Benjamin would interrogate the prisoners separately to be sure of what they told him was the truth. If the information did not match what the others had told him, he knew he was being deceived.

Once when his company was asked to escort some provision carts Benjamin secured some other men to guard the carts on their journey, while he and his men went on ahead to the destination point and lay an ambush along the path in case a party of the enemy had intentions of trying to attack and plunder the provision carts.

Church would never leave a place upon the same path he entered instead he would always choose another route out of an area so that he could not be ambushed by his enemies. He would also sent scouts out before moving to see if anyone had been following their party, or for signs of another force being nearby. When his company encamped, sentries were always posted, usually six men of which two at a time would keep watch on the paths leading to their encampment. Two men would also watch over the main body as they ate or slept. If they felt that an enemy might be near, they camped without fires so they would not be discovered.

When the company marched it did so spread apart as the natives did it this way. Once when Church asked some natives that he had captured how they were so successful in attacking the English parties as they marched, the natives told him they always marched thin and scattered, while the English marched in a heap, bunched so close together they could be hit with ease. The natives said they always knew that when an English party marched they always did in one party, never spread out, so the Indians did not have to worry about any other soldiers when they attacked. The natives also would scatter when attacked, while the English would bunch even tighter together. To help maintain order and silence while on the march the natives would call to each other using the sound an animal would make, or a low whistle instead of calling out.

When an enemy was discovered Church told his men not to immediately attack them, but rather to watch them undiscovered and wait until the morning to attack. Another time the enemy was discovered encamped within a small swamp. Church ordered some of his party to pass on both sides of the swamp and set an ambush on the other side. A party was also left at the entrance to the swamp in case any of the enemy tried to escape in that direction.

Church and his company used these skills and tactics to capture hundreds of natives. The main army of the confederated colonies was still in the field as well, putting pressure on the remaining natives still on the warpath. King Philip and his ever dwindling followers were constantly on the run trying to avoid capture. Food was scarce and the natives were subsisting on whatever they could find in the wilderness, or upon livestock they could steal and kill.

Benjamin had returned to Rhode Island to refresh and rest his men from their exhausting pursuit of the enemy when two men came up to him with the news that a native deserter had informed them that King Philip was nearby, and that the deserter would lead them to him. Gathering his company back together, Benjamin once again took off in pursuit of his foe. Philip was encamped with his followers on a rising piece of ground near a swamp, which Philip was sure to try and escape into when attacked. Church and some of his company would go and take their places at the swamp to try and capture anyone who tried to run there, while the other part of his force would crawl upon their bellies towards Philip's camp. Suddenly a gunshot was heard followed by a volley of gunfire. The attackers had been discovered and Philip, throwing up powder horn and shot bag over his head, picked up his musket and headed for the swamp. In the ensuing battle King Philip was shot and killed by one of the native members of Church's company. Only a small number of the natives escaped, including King Philip's War Captain, Annawon. Benjamin and his men returned in triumph to Rhode Island with King Philip's head, for which the native who killed him received thirty shillings.

After receiving the grateful thanks of the Plymouth Colony for their efforts, but little else, Church would once again lead his company out in search of Annawon, and any more of King Philip's confederates that were still at large. Benjamin and his men were able to surround Annawon and all of his party, including his son, making them his prisoners. Another of Philip's trusted warriors, Tuspaquin, turned himself in to Benjamin after Church had captured his wife and son. The native rebellion was dying out rapidly.

Benjamin would gather his company together to scour the countryside for any remaining natives in the coming months, but other than a few raids and skirmishes, King Philip's War was effectively over and things began to return to somewhat normal across New England, but this would not last long.

War between France and Great Britain would begin in Europe and become known as "King William's War" in North America. French and Indian raiders were soon attacking the settlements along the frontier of New England, striking fear into its inhabitants. Benjamin Church and his Rangers would be called upon once again to defend the colonies.

Church was summoned first to Boston to wait upon the Governor of Massachusetts, Sir Edmond Andross, who was not well liked in his administration of the office. The Governor asked Benjamin to accompany him on a campaign against the native tribes to the east that had been raiding and pillaging settlements in Maine, New Hampshire, and Massachusetts, because of his former good service in King Philip's War. Benjamin at this time was not overly enthused about the thought of war, especially under the present circumstances, and declined the offer. It was not much longer that a change in Government occurred in Massachusetts, and Simon Bradstreet was appointed Governor. Benjamin was requested to come to Boston to wait upon Governor Bradstreet, who asked for Church's assistance in the war effort. The circumstances this time were more to Benjamin's likes and with his sense of duty and honor returning, he accepted.

This time Church would be commissioned a Major, and would not be in command of just his own company, but as Commander in Chief of several independent companies who would operate as rangers in the woodland style of fighting. His own Plymouth Colony company, which would again be a mixed force of both English soldiers and allied natives, and two companies from the Massachusetts Colony under the command of Captain's Nathaniel Hall and Simon Willard, would serve under him. Benjamin also received agreements from the Massachusetts, Maine, and the Plymouth Colony assuring him of any needed assistance, and authorizing him to impress provisions, ammunition, watercraft, and any other items deemed necessary for the success of his military objectives. Wages and the rights to any captured goods were established for his men, including the sum of eight pounds per head for every fighting Indian killed by his rangers, as well as what was expected of the men in terms of their discipline and actions while under his command. Church was also ordered to observe and care for the men's worship of God with morning and evening prayers.

Church's targets were the Kennebeck Indians and other eastern tribes who had been committing atrocities against the English Settlements. These tribes were coming down from Canada into Maine, and then withdrawing back into Canada with their plunder and prisoners in tow. Church and his small army boarded two armed sloops that had been provided to take him and his men to their intended headquarters at Fort Casco, near the settlement of Falmouth in the territory of Maine. After securing the area Church and his forces would undertake offensive strikes against the enemy.

Sailing into Casco Harbor they were approached by three smaller ships already there. Not knowing if they were friend or foe Benjamin ordered his men to arms and prepared the guns of the sloops in case of attack. The ships turned out to contain their countrymen, who gave him the news that a large body of the enemy, as many as seven hundred, were on their way to attack the fort and town. Going ashore Benjamin found the fort in sad shape defensively, so he ordered that his men, after waiting until it turned dark, be disembarked from the sloops with as little noise as possible. He also ordered all able bodied men and Indians in town to prepare themselves for battle with shot bags and powder horns for their ammunition, as well as to look to their weapons to be sure they were well fixed for the coming enemy. When not enough shot bags and horns were available, a type of wallet was made that when folded in the middle, one side would hold powder, while the other held shot.

Instead of trying to defend the fort, Church ordered his men out into the woods an hour before daybreak so his men would be there before the native's traditional time of attack at sunrise. He positioned his men so that they would face the approach of the enemy, who hopefully unaware of the arrival of Church's men would walk into the carefully laid trap. While out with his men Benjamin discovered that most of the bullets issued to his troops were of musket size instead of the lighter bore size of many of the firelocks used by his men. He hurried back into the fort and ordered all of the casks of bullets onboard the sloops be brought to shore and dumped out on the ground in order to find smaller shot for his men. While he was there the sound of battle reached his ears, coming from the direction of where he had placed his forces. The approaching enemy had come in contact with his men, and a great battle soon began across a river near the fort. Rushing to the scene he found that several of his companies had been unable to cross the river before the battle started, and were firing from the far side of the river at the enemy. Church asked some of the local soldiers if there was any other way of crossing the river, to which they replied that there was a bridge nearby that they could use to cross the river. Calling to some of his natives, Church started out to find the bridge telling his men to cross it "spread out and thin" in case any of the enemy waited there to ambush anyone trying to cross over. Church and his natives, if they could get across the bridge, meant to get in the rear of the enemy and attack them as they were engaged with his men in front. Finding no one at the bridge, but evidence that the enemy had been there, Church and his natives quickly took to the woods in search of them. Finding none, they noticed that the firing from the front was quieting down; Benjamin assumed that either the enemy had withdrawn, or they were trying to find another approach to the fort. Scouring the surrounding woods and brush they found none of the enemy, and they soon learned that they had indeed withdrawn when they ran in such strong resistance. Church and his men returned to the fort carrying their wounded and dead. The townspeople were very exuberant in their praise of Major Church and his army, saying that God had sent them as their saviors because they could not have survived an attack from so great an enemy. In fact, this was the first time that the eastern Indians had been repelled in any of their raids against the settlements for as long as anyone could remember.

It was now very late in the year so Benjamin was ordered to check the other smaller English posts in Maine to see that they were in good order, leave troops there to garrison them, and return with the remainder of his army to Boston. The inhabitants of Casco were much distressed that Church and his men were leaving, but before he left Benjamin promised that he would return again in the spring to defend them.

Arriving in Boston, Benjamin waited upon the government there to plead the case of the inhabitants at Casco as he had promised. After waiting upon them for some time, and beginning to lose his patience, he was finally able to give his recommendations to the assembly. Church related that the inhabitants were more than willing to fight for their King, but must have sufficient aid and manpower in order to withstand any assaults by their enemies coming towards them from Canada, such as the service performed by Major Church. Benjamin advised the council that if they decided not to give this desired aid, the settlement must then be abandoned and the fort destroyed as they could not help but fall prey to the enemy without the requested aid. If the post was abandoned, it would at least keep the arms and other military supplies there from falling into enemy hands. Taking Benjamin's advice under consideration, but giving him no answer, Church was given permission to disband his troops and return home.

In May of the following Spring Benjamin would learn that no decision had been made and that as expected, the inhabitants of Casco had been cut off and massacred by a raiding party of Eastern Indians. These natives had been supplied for this raid by the French, and were commanded on this strike against the English by a Frenchman, Monsieur Casteen, who allowed the savages to butcher most of the English inhabitants. This news was a real blow to Benjamin. He had been treated very fairly by the people at Casco Harbor, and was sad to hear of the devastation of the settlement there. It was not a fitting end after the success he and his men had enjoyed there in their first campaign of King William's War.

In the spring of 1690 the French and Eastern Indians were once again raiding the provinces of Maine, New Hampshire, and Massachusetts. They were successful in capturing the English stone fort at Pejepscot, and captured many prisoners. The confederated colonies wanted Benjamin to again raise his independent companies to protect their territories from depredations by the enemy, but to also go and attack the enemy in their own territories. Church at first was reluctant to go because of what had happened to the settlement at Casco, when the War Council did not heed his advice and let the people there be slaughtered, but the colonies persisted until Benjamin relented and agreed to raise his Company and set out for Maine to pursue the enemy. Church was again commissioned Major and Commander in Chief of the forces enlisted for this duty. After waiting some time for the promised supplies and ships for transport to Maine, Benjamin and his army set sail.

Upon arrival Church and his men set out for the native fort at Pejepscot, but found nothing there. They then started marching to Amerascogen, a beautiful river in New Hampshire where another enemy fort stood. As they came near the fort they spied an Indian and his wife with two English captives. Giving chase the men fired at the fleeing natives and the wife was shot and killed, allowing the two captives to gain their freedom. The fleeing male Indian ran straight to the fort and the other warriors inside quickly fled, leaving their women and children and some captives behind. The enemy warriors ran down to the river and the falls that were there and escaped. Benjamin ordered his men to destroy the corn fields found there, except for a little corn which was saved for the sustenance of their prisoners. Interrogating the prisoners taken in the fort

Benjamin was informed that the natives were waiting on the arrival of some Indians from the Bay of Fundy to come and help them fight the English, and most of their warriors were out getting provisions with which to feed these new arrivals. Ranging across the area surrounding the river, Church and his men came upon a party of the enemy, and during a smart skirmish were able to drive them away. Some of church's officers, now that they had taken some plunder, were of the mind that they should return home, and others even claimed to be sick. Benjamin was against it, stating that the enemy was sure to return, and that they should stay and do their duty as ordered. A council of war was held and Church was out voted, forcing him to embark with his army aboard their transport vessels. As they boarded the boats, several canoes full of the enemy came into sight which quickly turned around at the sight of the ships, returning up the river the way they had come. They set sail and during the course of the night one of the ships ran aground. After it was freed, they continued on using one of their captive natives as a guide on the river. That night they anchored the ships in the river, but with the vessels being so crowded, Church, and three companies of his men went on shore to spend the night. Finding a house and two barns nearby for the troops to lodge in, Major Church set out to return to the boats. In doing so he ran into a group of his own native allies going to shore to spend the night there also. Benjamin warned them not to make any fires, but by morning they had done so, and were singing and dancing around them. Knowing that the enemy would have seen these fires and likely were on their way to attack the English forces, Benjamin ordered a boat to be hauled up to take him to shore to warn the men staying in the house and barns of the danger. Just as the Major was about to enter the boat, the enemy attacked his men on the shore. Quickly assembling all of the fighting men left onboard the vessels they landed as fast as they could get to shore and engaged the enemy. The battle was very intense, but soon died down as the enemy melted away into the forest. Embarking all of his men, including the dead and wounded from this fight aboard the transports, they continued their journey home, at which time Benjamin traveled to Boston to inform the counsel of the specifics of his second expedition against the eastern Indians.

While in Boston Benjamin was almost destitute having only eight pence to his name and his clothes were nearly worn out from the hard use they had seen during the campaign. The men of the council seemed to be displeased with him for some reason unknown to him, and when he asked to borrow some funds to see him home with, they refused him.

Walking from Boston to Roxbury because he had no funds for travel, Church ran into an old friend from Rohde Island who loaned him the money to get home. Benjamin's brother Caleb also arrived with a spare horse and Benjamin was finally able to reach his home. Being confused about his treatment in Boston, Church would write to the men of the council to see if he could find out what had caused this treatment. He soon found out that some of his officers had cast rumors about him saying that Benjamin had allowed his men to commit sinful acts while on the expedition against the eastern tribes, had killed some cattle, and after putting the meat in barrels, he then sold it in Boston for his own profit. With the cloud of these accusations hanging over his head Church's second mission to Maine ended on a very sour note.

In 1692 Benjamin was once again summoned to Boston, only this time it was to wait on Sir William Phips, who after the ascension of King William and Queen Mary to the English Throne, was named Captain General and Governor of the Province of Massachusetts Bay. He offered Benjamin a commission as Major for an expedition against the eastern Indians that he would lead himself, and that in his absence, Church would become Commander in Chief of the army in his stead. Having incurred serious debts for the last two campaigns, and being promised that he would be richly rewarded for his service, Church accepted.

Assembling his mixed companies of English and natives, the army set off bound for Pemequid, in the province of Maine. Stopping off at Casco Harbor they began to bury the bones of the massacred settlers that had lain in the open since the attack, as well as to haul off the large artillery pieces still inside the destroyed fort. Moving on to the harbor at Pemequid, Sir Phips told Benjamin that he had special orders from the King to build a new fort there, and wanted all but one of Church's companies to stay there and work on the construction. Benjamin instead begged that he be allowed to take two of his companies and travel on to Penobscot in search of the enemy. The Governor granted this request and gave Church the following orders before his men and he left.

"Whereas you are Major, and so chief officer of a body of men detached out of the militia, appointed for an expedition against the French and Indian enemies; you are duly to observe the following instructions:

Imprimis, You are to take care that the worship of God be duly and constantly maintained and kept up among you; and to suffer no swearing, cursing, or other profanation of the holy name of God: and, as much as in you lies, to deter and hinder all the other vices among your soldiers.

"2dly, You are to proceed with the soldiers under your command, to Penobscot, and, with what privacy and undiscoverable methods you can, there to land your men, and take the best measures to surprise the enemy.

"3dly, You are by killing, destroying, and all other means possible, to endeavour the destruction of the enemy, in pursuance whereof, being satisfied of your courage and conduct, I leave the same to your discretion.

"4thly, You are to endeavour the taking what captives you can, either men, women, or children, and the same safely to keep and convey them unto me.

"5thly, Since it is not possible to judge how affairs may be circumstanced with you there, I shall therefore not limit your return, but leave it to your prudence, only that you make no longer stay than you can improve for advantage against the enemy, or may reasonably hope for the same.

"6thly, You are also to take care and be very industrious by all means to find out and destroy all the enemy's corn, and other provisions in all places where you can come at the same.

"7thly, You are to return from Penobscot and the Eastern parts, to make all dispatch hence for Kennebeck river, and the places adjacent, and there prosecute all advantages against the enemy as aforesaid.

" 8thly, If any soldier, officer, or other shall be disobedient to you as their Commander in Chief, or other superior officer, or make, or cause, any mutiny, commit other offences or disorders, you shall call a council of war among your officers, and having tried him or them so offending, inflict such punishment as the merit of the offense requires, death only excepted, which, if any shall deserve, you are to secure the person, and signify the crime unto me by the first opportunity.

"Given under my hand, this 11th day of August, 1692. WILLIAM PHIPS." (Church, 177, 178)

Setting out for Penobscot' Benjamin and his men captured two Frenchmen who lived in the area with their native wives and children. Examining them for information, Church soon learned that a large number of the enemy were on a nearby island. Asking his prisoners to show him where anyone on the island normally crossed over to the main land, Benjamin had his men set an ambush at the site. Soon enough a canoe containing an Indian man and women fell into their trap. Capturing these prisoners without being discovered by the remaining Indians on the island, He sent for the rest of his men in case the any more of the enemy would be crossing over as well. The men, instead of coming quietly to the ambush site through the woods, instead traveled right up the river in plain sight of the island, whereby the enemy discovered them and started to flee in their canoes. Not having enough boats to try and pursue them with, Benjamin could only watch as his enemy disappeared down the river. Church swore then and there that he would never go to war again without a number of whaleboats on hand in order to always be prepared to pursue the enemy upon the water.

Church then, according to his instructions, had his men scour the area destroying all the corn and provisions they could find, as well as any canoes, which they readily did. Running low on food, they returned to Pemequid, where they found the Governor just preparing to leave for Boston to provide more provisions for the army. Before he left the Governor ordered Benjamin to the Kennebeck River in search of the enemy in accordance to his previous orders to do as much mischief against them as possible. When they accomplished what they could at Kennebeck, they were to return to Pemequid and help with the building of the fort there until his return.

Upon reaching the Kennebeck River, Church and his men ranged the area looking for the enemy, which they soon found and a battle was engaged. The enemy was driven off after a hard fight in which they natives abandoned their canoes, and instead took flight through the woods towards their village, with Benjamin and his party hot on their heels. Driving the enemy from the village, they set the town ablaze and destroyed several cribs of picked corn there. Being very low on provisions Church had no choice but to return to Pemequid and set his men to working on the construction of the fort as ordered.

The Governor returned with fresh provisions, but hardly enough to sustain another expedition against the enemy in the area, so the army set sail and returned to Boston. Instead of being richly rewarded as promised, Benjamin actually went into debt another twelve pounds for his service to the colony. Church would have been money ahead to have stayed at home.

In 1696 Benjamin Church was in Boston as he was now a member of the House of Representatives, and while there, the General Court, in response to continuing attacks by the French and Indians from the east against the colonies, requested that Benjamin raise his companies of rangers to go out and attack the enemy in an effort to stop their raiding. Church told them if he and his men were provided with all the necessaries for the mission, including some whale boats, he would raise the needed men. His commission and orders were much the same as his last, so Benjamin assembled his army at Boston in preparation to sail out towards his intended targets.

While at Boston news came in with some prisoners of war that the French and Indians had attacked and captured the fort just built at Pemequid, destroyed the fortifications there, and after taking all of the artillery and military stores, returned with them to the St. John's River, where the French planned to build a fort and outfit it with the English guns and stores taken from Pemequid.

Hoping to catch the French and Indians before they scattered, Church at once set out for the Piscataqua River, (Near the border of present day New Hampshire and Maine). Church had been given information that a French sloop was in the region, so he thought that the enemy may have gone there after destroying the fort. Arriving at Piscataqua, Church sent off some of his native soldiers to scout the area around York in search of the enemy. Having no luck in finding either the French sloop or any of the enemy, Benjamin tried a new tactic in an effort to discover his foe.

Taking the whaleboats provided to him, Church and his men would row around the waterways at night looking for the fires of any enemy encampments. Church and his men would take to land before daylight, hiding their boats, and then would rest during the day, keeping men watching the water for any of the enemy traveling upon it in the daylight. They found the remnants of old camps, but did not find any new sign of the enemy. Being informed by one of their river guides that 50 or 60 miles upriver a large Indian village stood, they decided to go and try to attack the town undiscovered. Arriving at the village, they found it deserted, and no provisions or other goods there. Church sent his men out to range the surrounding woods searching for the enemy, leaving men posted on both sides of the river to watch for anyone traveling upon it. Presently a canoe with two Indians in it appeared, who were to be taken prisoner so they could be interrogated, but one of the soldiers fired at them too early, spoiling the ambush. The Indians, although wounded, managed to escape. Suddenly three more Indians in another canoe came into sight upon the river and were fired upon. The enemy beached their canoe and escaped into the woods. Knowing that these men would spread the word that the English were downstream, it would do Church and his men no good to proceed further upstream. Hoping to still find some of the enemy in order to carry out his instructions against them, Benjamin ordered his men to make their way back to their transports, and proceed to Penobscot bay. Arriving there they found some abandoned villages and destroyed some corn fields, but the enemy could not be found. Having a council of war the officers determined to go as far east as necessary in search of the enemy, which accordingly they did, ranging through the woods and swamps finding a few Indians, but they concluded that the enemy must have gotten some knowledge of their coming, and had departed before the army arrived, (which they would later find out had indeed been the case).

The army now thought about going over to the St John's River in Nova Scotia because of the information they had that the French were building a fort there, and had another a little way up the river. The Captains of the Transport ships would not agree to go because there were reported to be several strong French ships present, so instead, Benjamin took his troops to Senactaca Bay where a village of the enemy stood, and some Frenchmen lived. Arriving at the village around sunrise, they were seen by the enemy, who took up their goods and fled into the woods after firing a few shots at the incoming ships. A Frenchmen was captured who refused to talk. Church ordered his men to range the woods in search of the enemy and to try to take prisoners if possible, which they did, and became engaged in a skirmish with some French and Indians, who escaped after firing at Church's men. They did capture a couple of Frenchmen who pledged to help Church and his men if their homes and families were not hurt, which Benjamin agreed too. In their ranging the soldiers found some gun powder and shot belonging to the natives. They also confiscated several barrels of gun powder, shot, and other weapons from a French trader who had been supplying them to the natives. The troops burned the native village, and having done all they could do there, they determined what and where to go next.

Finally convincing the transport ships Captains to go and attack the fort being built at St. Johns, they embarked aboard the vessels and set sail for the river. Landing his troops a little distance from the mouth of the river, Church and his men traveled through the woods in order to surprise the men working there. Seeing the men at work, and the rest of the enemy forces across on the other side of the river, Church ordered his men back to the boats to plan his attack. All of the boats would sail for the mouth of the river where Church and his men would land and rush against the enemy, which the next morning they did, under heavy firing from the French, but which did no real damage. The French and the natives there were forced to abandon their canoes and flee into the woods. A wounded French Corporal was captured, who begged that his wound be treated, and if they did, he would tell them the hiding places of the artillery and goods taken from the fort at Pemequid. Church recovered the twelve guns that had been taken, as well as their carriages, powder, and shot, along with some pork and flour stored in barrels, Church questioned his prisoners about the whereabouts of any more of the enemy. Being told that they were entrenched at another fort further up the river into Canada, the men, not being willing to take on such a expedition, after such a long campaign as they had already undertaken, voted to continue where they were in search of anymore of their foe.

So Church and his men continued to range the woods while the artillery and stores that they had recovered were loaded aboard the ships. Benjamin's men found a French Shallop anchored in a creek, which they took possession of thinking it might be useful in their efforts against the enemy. Some of the enemy were taken captive, but finding few others, the officer's determined that they should return home having done a great deal to thwart the enemy in their attacks against the colonies, and so they set sail for home.

In their passage they met with three of His Majesty's Ships, one of them being a Man of War with Colonel Hathorne on board. They had been ordered to attack the French at St. Johns, and the Colonel had orders aboard his ship for Major Church to accompany him on this expedition. Explaining to the Colonel that he and his men had already driven off the enemy from the fortifications they were building there, and had recovered the munitions taken from the fort at Pemequid, he could still not prevail upon the Colonel to abandon his mission, the Colonel stating that he had his orders and must obey them. Benjamin had no choice but to follow these orders as well. Going back to St. Johns they of course found none of the enemy. Benjamin did find an English man who had been taken from Marblehead and had recently escaped his captors. He told Benjamin that all of the natives in the area had fled to the north when they were informed that Church and his men were coming against them. The trip back to St. John's had done little more than to increase the fatigue which Church and his men felt after so long and hard a campaign.

Returning to Boston Benjamin once again met with disappointment. The assembly there took possession of the artillery and munitions recovered by Church's men not giving them any reward for it, and sought to reduce his own and his men's pay to half, which was only stopped at the insistence of Lt. Governor Stoughton.

King William's War would end with peace being established between England and France in 1697. His fourth expedition against the French and Indians to the east, although having met with great success, would again leave Benjamin more in debt than when he had first started out from Boston.

King William of England passed away and his wife's sister Anne ascended the throne as Queen. War once again broke out between France and England. "Queen Anne's War" as it was known on the American continent started much the same as the earlier conflicts. French and Indian raiding parties again descended upon the New England countryside destroying homes and lives as they went. The massacre of the settlement of Deerfield, Massachusetts in 1704 was particularly horrific, such that when Benjamin Church learned of the atrocities committed there he became so enraged that he went down to wait upon his Excellency, Joseph Dudley, who was Captain General and Governor in Chief of the Provinces of Massachusetts Bay and New Hampshire, offering his services in the coming campaign.

Dudley instructed Church to put together a plan of action and return these to him as soon as possible. The following are Benjamin's specific recommendations for the expedition against their French and Indian enemies.

"1st, That ten or twelve hundred good able soldiers, well equipped, be in readiness fit for action by the first of April at farthest, for then will be the time to be upon action.

"2dly, That five and forty or fifty good whaleboats be had ready, well fitted, with five good oars, and twelve or fifteen good paddles to each boat; and upon the wale of each boat five pieces of strong leather be fastened on each side, to slip five strong ash bars through, so that, whenever they land, the men may step overboard, and slip in said bars across, and take up said boat, that she may not be hurt against the rocks; and that two suitable brass kettles be provided to belong to each boat, to cook the men's victuals in, to make their lives comfortable.

"3dly, That four or five hundred pair of good Indian shoes be made ready, fit for the service, for the English and Indians, that must improve the whale-boats, and birch canoes, for they will be very proper, and safe for that service; and let there be a good store of cow-hides, well tanned, for a supply of such shoes; and hemp to make thread, and wax, to mend and make more such shoes as wanted, and a good store of awls.

"4thly, That there be an hundred large hatchets, or light axes, made pretty broad, and steeled with the best steel that can be gotten, (and made by workmen, that they may cut well, and hold, that the hemlock knots may not break or turn them,) to widen the landing place up the falls, for it may happen that we may get up, with some of our whale-boats, to their falls or headquarters.

"5thly, That there be a suitable quantity of small bags, or wallets provided, that every man that wants may have one, to put up his bullets in, of such size as will fit his gun, and not be served as at Casco. That every man's bag be so marked that he may not change it. For if so, it will make a great confusion in action. That every man's store of ball be weighed to him, that so he may be accountable, and may not squander it away. And also his store of powder, that so he may try his powder and gun before action. And that every particular company may have a barrel of powder to themselves, and so marked that it may by no means be changed; that men may know before hand, and may not be cheated out of their lives, by having bad powder; or not knowing how to use it. This will prove a great advantage to the action.

"6thly, That Col. John Gorham, if he may be prevailed with, may be concerned in the management of the whale-boats, being formerly concerned in the eastern parts, and experienced in that affair. And whale-men will be very serviceable in this expedition, which having a promise made to them, that they shall be released in good season, to go whaling in the fall, your Excellency will have men enough.

"7thly, That there may be raised for this service three hundred Indians at least, and more of if they may be had; for I know certainly of my own knowledge, that they exceed most of our English in hunting and skulking in the woods, being always used to it; and it must be practised if we ever intend to destroy those Indian enemies.

" 8thly, That the soldiers already out eastward in the service, men of known judgment, may take a survey of them and their arms; and see if their arms be good, and that they know how to use them, in shooting right at a mark; and that they be men of good reason and sence, to know how to manage themselves in so difficult a piece of service, as this Indian hunting is; for bad men are but a clogg and hindrance to an army, being a trouble and vexation to good commanders, and so many mouths to devour the country's provision, and a hindrance to all good action.

"9thly, That special care be had in taking up the whale-boats, that they be good and fit for that service; so that the country be not cheated, as formerly, in having rotten boats; and as much care that the owners may have good satisfaction for them.

"10thly, That tenders or transports, vessels to be improved in this action, be decked vessels, not too big, because of going up several rivers; having four or six small guns apiece for defence, and fewer men will defend them; and there are enough such vessels to be had.

"11thly, To conclude all, if your Excellency will be pleased to make yourself great, and us a happy people, as to the destroying of our enemies, and easing of our taxes, &c. be pleased to draw forth all those forces now in pay in all eastward parts, both at Saco and Casco Bay; for those two trading houses never did any good, nor ever will, and are not worthy the name of Queen's forts; and the first building of them had no other effect that to lay us under tribute to the wretched pagan crew, and I hope they will never be wanted for what they were first built. But sure it is, they are very serviceable to them, for they get many a good advantage of us to destroy our men, and laugh at us for our folly, that we should be at so much cost and trouble to do a thing that does us so much harm, and no manner of good. But to the contrary, when they see all of our forces drawn forth, and in pursuit of them, they will think that we begin to be roused up, and to be awakened, and will not be satisfied with what they have pleased to leave us, but are resolved to retake from them what they formerly took from us, and drive them out of their country also. The which being done, then to build a fort at a suitable time, and in a convenient place; and it will be very honorable to your Excellency, and of great service to her Majesty, and to the enlargement of her Majesty's government. The place meant at Port Royal.

"12thly, That the objection made against drawing off the forces in the eastward parts will be no damage to the inhabitants; for former experience teaches us, that so soon as drawn into their country, they will presently forsake ours to care for their own. That there will be no failure in making preparation of these things aforementioned, (for many times the want of small things prevents the completing of great actions;) and that everything be in readiness before the forces be raised, to prevent charges, and the enemy having intelligence. And that the General Court be moved to make suitable acts for encouraging both English and Indians; that so men of business may freely offer estates and concerns to serve the public."(Church, 210-213)

The Governor approved of all of Benjamin's recommendations except for the expedition against the French at Port Royal, Acadia. Dudley expressed support for the mission, but told Church that he would have to get the approval of the Queen before he could order such action. Accordingly, the Governor commissioned Church to be Colonel and Commander in Chief of the forces enlisted for this expedition, and charged him with the destruction of the enemy to the east.

Church and his army set sail for Piscataqua where he and his men left the transports in their whale-boats with provisions for several days. The army ranged the countryside with good results capturing many prisoners and military stores which were loaded upon the transport ships. During these scouts a Frenchman and his two sons were captured. Interrogating the men proved difficult, so Benjamin ordered brush to be gathered and threatened to burn the sons at the stake if they did not give him knowledge of the whereabouts of the enemy, a strategy he had used with great success before. The men, fearing greatly for their lives, told Benjamin everything he needed to know, specifically the location of large number of the enemy at Passamequado Harbor.

Arriving at their destination, Church and his men landed and began to scour the area. In doing so they captured some prisoners who told them that a large group of warriors were up the river at the falls fishing. Leaving part of his men stationed on two islands in the river to watch for any sign of the enemy, Benjamin and the rest of his party went up the river towards the falls. In a skirmish with the natives there, they forced the enemy to flee and destroyed the stores of fish that they had caught. It was very late in the season, and there would not be another time in which to make such a large catch, so this was a great discouragement to the enemy.

Continuing along the river they captured several French people who gave them the intelligence of a large number of the enemy at the town of Menis, which was close by the French post at Port Royal. Ordering his war ships and transports to sail towards Port Royal, Church and his men would go in their whale-boats to the town at Menis in search of the enemy, then rendezvous with the ships for a possible assault on Port Royal.

The enemy forces at Menis were warned of the approach of Church and his men by some of the natives who had escaped them at Passamequado. Church in approaching the town sent word that he had the place surrounded and demanded the surrender of the post, but the French and Indians came down to where he and his men were and started firing at them from the safety of the nearby woods. Benjamin was aboard a whale-boat which had a small cannon fixed upon it. He ordered it charged with bags of shot, which were fired at the enemy in the woods. This shot made much noise as it spread out and rattled among the trees, and caused the enemy to take to flight. Church and his men took possession of the town as well as taking many prisoners and goods found there. Church released some of his prisoners telling them to go to the French Governor in Canada and warn him not to send anymore raiding parties, such as the one that struck Deerfield, or Church would return with a great army and lay waste to the French homes just as they had done at Deerfield. Then, having destroyed all of the cornfields in the area, and destroying the dams that the enemy had built in order prevent the tides from coming in and drowning their crops, as well as all other provisions that they could find, they left for the rendezvous with his ships to attack Port Royal.

Upon meeting his ships Benjamin soon learned that the French garrison at Port Royal was very strong and alert to their intentions of attacking them, and so it was decided that they were not a large enough force to attempt such an enterprise. Having done all they felt they could do, the officers were all of the opinion that they should return home, which Benjamin readily agreed to. It would be the last campaign of Benjamin Church's military career.

Benjamin was in his mid sixties when he led this last expedition, and starting to falter a bit in the woods due to his advanced age to the point that he had to be helped over downed trees and other obstacles he encountered on the way to Menis. Nevertheless he was an able commander, though upon returning to Boston he was once again not well compensated for his service to the colonies.

Benjamin Church would die when he was 78 years old after a fall from his horse. He was one of the first Englishmen to promote the use of mixed units of colonists and natives, operating as rangers, and fighting in the native style, and be successful at it. Benjamin Church can be rightly called the "Father of the Rangers."

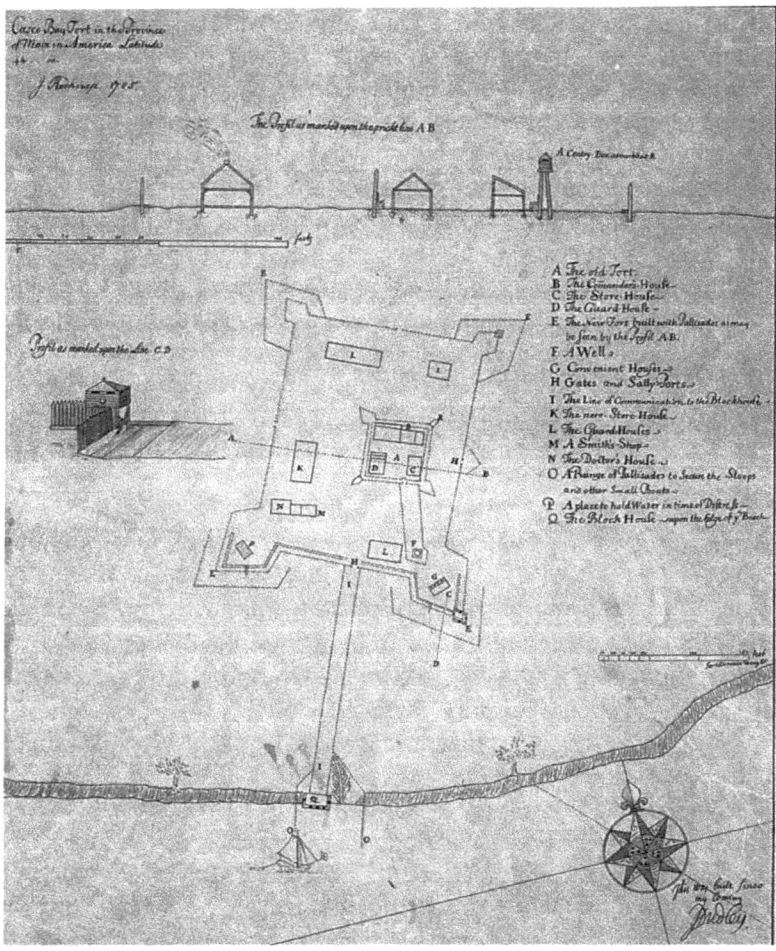

This drawing shows the English fort at Casco Bay in 1705. This larger fort was built to replace the one destroyed by the French and Indians during King William's War. The outline of the original and much smaller fort can be seen inside the new one. This drawing is in the collection the Raymond H. Folger Library at the University of Maine and is used with permission by the "Windows on Maine" Educational Project for Teachers and people interested in the History of Maine.

New England Snowshoe Men

In February of 1704 the Governor of New France, Pierre de Rigaud Marquis de Vaudreuil, sent out a mixed force of two hundred Huron, Mohawk, and Abenaki Indians, along with approximately fifty French and Canadian soldiers under the command of Jean-Baptiste Hertel de Rouville, on a raiding mission into the New England Colonies. Some of these Indians were "Christianized," having been converted to the faith by French Catholic Missionaries. The force left Canada in bitterly cold weather on snowshoes with sleds pulled by dogs loaded with provisions towards their target, the settlement of Deerfield, Massachusetts. This small town, which was a group of houses surrounding a wooden stockade in the center of the settlement, which itself contained several buildings and homes inside, had long been the victim of attacks by French and Indian raiders dating back to before King William's War. Being situated on the frontier of Massachusetts, it was a natural place to attack.

The cold weather and deep snow did little to hamper the raiders, who being used to travel in these conditions by their daily existence in Canada, were very well adapted to such hardship. Arriving before Deerfield at nightfall, the French and Indians built shelters in the snow, huddling together without fires, so that they would not be discovered while they waited for just before dawn to launch their attack. The small garrison maintained at Deerfield had either posted no sentries, possibly because they felt they were safe from an attack in the present weather, or the watch had fallen asleep. Scouts sent to look over the town came back stating that all was quiet and no one was stirring.

The weather would actually help the attackers in that the snow had piled up so high against the walls of the stockade that it allowed the raiders to simply walk up to the top of the wall and drop over the edge to the inside. Opening the gates the French and Indians stormed inside, while others in their party attacked the surrounding houses. The enemy seemed to be everywhere, killing townspeople and setting fire to the buildings. The surprise was near complete except for a group of settlers that gathered together and fortified themselves inside the Stebbins house, holding off their assailants until a militia group from a nearby settlement, seeing the smoke of the burning buildings, came to their aid.

This small relief force was no match for the raiders and suffered many casualties in their attempt to aid the town. It did however force the French and Indians to decide to gather their prisoners and plunder and begin their long withdrawal back to Canada before any more help arrived. Many of the Deerfield inhabitants tried to escape by running away from the town in an attempt to reach the safety of nearby settlements. Most were still dressed in their night clothes and suffered greatly in their escape.

Fifty six townspeople were killed in the attack, including women and children. During the three hundred mile journey back to Canada another twenty one would die of exposure in the harsh weather, or be killed by their captors because they could not keep up with the rapid pace set because the raiders feared that they might be pursued. Survivors of the grueling march told of children being snatched from the arms of their mothers and tomahawked or smashed against trees. Eventually some of the captives would be returned to their homes when they were traded for French captives in English hands, or their families paid to ransom them back.

"The Deerfield Massacre," as it would become known because of the particularly horrific atrocities that the raiders committed, brought a very real fear into the New England settlements. The Massachusetts Colony was assailed by their inhabitants to do something to prevent such attacks.

This image is an original woodcut print showing the Deerfield Massacre. The Native American raiders are shown surrounding one of the large houses in the town. This image is public domain and is taken from Wikipedia, the Free Online Dictionary.

The usefulness of groups of rangers to scout given areas of the frontier in search of sign of an approaching enemy had been well established during King Philip's War, so Massachusetts naturally looked to these guardians of the frontier as an answer to the problem, but adapted to meet the needs of defense during the winter months.

The Massachusetts Government established rules requiring settlements along their frontiers to have a ready supply of snowshoes on hand at all times.

'The Use of Snow-shoes appearing very requisite for marching in the Winter season, occasioned an Act in both Provinces for supplying the Frontiers therewith: And this Season, which before was dreaded as most hazardous, was now the time of greatest safety, and of less difficulty in traveling." (Penhallow, 11)

Provincial Snowshoe Companies were formed made up of men who lived on the frontier, were used to traveling in the winter months, as well as being trained in the use of snowshoes. These companies would range over established territories of the colony to give warning of the approach of any enemy forces, so that the colony militias could muster for the defense of the settlements, and so that the settlers when warned could make their way to the blockhouses and other fortifications built throughout the colony as a safe place to gather in case of an enemy attack.

The necessity of having such men trained in the use of snowshoes, and a ready supply on hand was quite evident after the Deerfield Massacre. The day after the attack, men from around the area came in great numbers to the burned out settlement, but were unable to try and overtake the raiders because.

"But for want of Snow-shoes, were unable to pursue them." (Penhallow, 13)

These companies of snowshoe men would also undertake offensive strikes against their enemies in their own territory, but with an added goal. They would continue to seek out and destroy the enemy, but they would also be sent on missions into enemy territory to seek intelligence of what the enemy was doing, where their main encampments were, how many troops were in the field, and other needed information that could aid the English in making military decisions. These reconnaissance patrols would often be of just a few men to lessen the possibility of being discovered. It would do little good to travel into enemy territory and not make it back out safely with the information gathered.

The men chosen for the Snowshoe Companies were be able to sustain themselves out in the wilderness during their scouts, which at times could take them far from home and any source of supply other than what they could provide for themselves. Caleb Lyman was on such a scout in which they had engaged and killed several of the enemy. Upon taking stock of their situation and provisions after the battle, the men discovered that.

"We had not more than eno' for one small refreshment: and being above one hundred miles from any English settlement, we were very tho'tful how we should subsist by the way. For having tracked about thirty of the Enemy a little before us, we could not hunt for subsistence, for fear of Discovery: and so were obliged to eat Buds of tress, Grass, & Strawberry Leaves." (Penhallow, 22)

The Snowshoe men were of course induced to engage in this duty by the promise of scalp money, and the lure of plunder from any enemy they defeated.

"The General Assembly being sensibly affected with the state of matters, and disposed to a Vigorous prosecution of the War, enacted, that Forty Pounds should be given for every Indian Scalp, which prompted some, and animated others to a noble Emulation." (Penhallow, 10)

The men were also provided the following if they reached their enlistment quotas.

"To such should offer volunteers, they presented a good Firelock, Cartouch-box, Flints, Ammunition, a Coat, Hat and Shirt; with an assurance of her Majesty's Princely Favour unto all such as should distinguish themselves." (Penhallow, 50)

The French were of course also guilty of enticing the natives to attack the English settlements with presents and scalp money. A French ship was captured by a gunboat out of Virginia on its way to Canada, aboard which was found.

"Two thousand small arms, with Ammunition answerable, besides a vast number of Crucifixes, and Presents of a greater value for encouraging the Indians in their acts of Hostility against the English." (Penhallow, 14)

The Snowshoe Companies would provide a vital service during Queen Anne's War, as well as during Dummer's War in the 1720's. Men such as Seth Wyman, John White, John Lovewell, Samuel Willard, and Johnson Harmon would lead companies of snowshoe clad rangers into the snow covered wilderness in search of the enemy.

Captain Harmon would lead a party of 34 men to the Kennebeck River in 1722 in search of the enemy. Traveling by boat at night they saw the fires of an encampment in the dark. Landing upon the shore they started towards the location of the fires and soon came upon eleven canoes beached on the shoreline. Creeping forward the rangers came up to a group of Indians sleeping around a fire. The rangers attacked the Indians and in about ten minutes time had slain or driven the whole party off. The rangers recovered fifteen firelocks left behind by the natives in their haste to flee the attack, but the rangers would also make another, more gruesome discovery, first the hand, and then the rest of the body of an Englishman. He had been terribly tortured and his mangled body had been cut to pieces. Taking up the remains so they could be brought away and given a decent burial, the rangers were soon fired upon by another party of Indians who had come to investigate the noise of the initial attack. The firing from this party did no harm, and Captain Harmon and his men were able to return to their boats and retreat to safety.

During Dummer's War the Snowshoe Men would again be rewarded for scalps and whatever plunder they could take on their scouts, such as the fifteen firelocks captured above, but the General Assembly, in order to entice the men to fall out in the event of an attack by French and Indian raiders, also promised an additional thirty pounds reward to be paid to the companies that assembled, along with the established payment promised to the rangers

Just such an occurrence happened in September of 1722 when a large party of French and Indians attacked the garrison house at Arowsick. The areas inhabitants were mostly able to gather what belongings they could and make it to the safety of the garrison house before the Natives attacked it. The Indians surrounded the house and put up an almost continuous fire against it for several hours, wounding many of the defenders inside by shooting at them through the loopholes of the house. Captains Harmon and Walton assembled their men at the first alarm, and traveling to the garrison house in whaleboats, were able to drive the Indians away.

The snowshoe companies would continue their scouts and offensive strikes over the next several years, providing security and defense for the New England frontier. The companies executed their duties with such success the frontier went relatively unharmed during the winter season.

"During the Winter little or no spoil was done on any of our Frontiers; the Enemy being so terrified by reason of Snow-shoes (which most of our men were skilful in) that they never attempted coming at such a season after." (Penhallow, 32)

The Snowshoe Men would be called upon to defend the frontier once again during King George's War. In 1744 Governor Shirley raised ten companies of Snowshoe Men consisting of fifty men per company. He described their duties to the Duke of Newcastle as.

"To hold themselves ready at the shortest Warning to go in pursuit of any Party of Indians, who frequently in the time of War make sudden Incursions, whilst there is deep Snow upon the Ground, and retreat as suddenly into the Woods after having done what Mischief they can." (Grenier, 61)

The Snowshoe Men were also ordered to construct a line of blockhouses to be used in conjunction with their patrols for the defense of the frontier settlements. These winter warriors would serve with great distinction until the end of the war and the companies were disbanded.

Many a frontier settler would owe their lives to these rangers, who braved the bitter cold and snow of the New England winter to protect the English settlements.

The author has his toboggan packed and is ready for a snowshoe patrol, much like the New England Snowshoe Men.

John Lovewell's Rangers

In the early 1700's at the end of Queen Anne's War when peace had been established between France and England in Europe, small conflicts between the French and their Indian allies and the English continued to be waged in North America. In these years several small battles between the two enemies occurred because the English had begun to establish settlements along the Kennebeck River in present day Maine, and thereby lay claim to the territory for England. This was seen by the Abenaki Indians as an encroachment upon their lands, and with French aid, they began to raid the countryside burning homes, killing settlers, and taking captives. To try and protect the frontier from these raids the English built Fort Dummer in the Vermont territory, which led to this time of conflict being called "Dummer's War."

These raids could be very lucrative for the natives. The goods they took during these raids, weapons included, could be sold, or kept for their own use. Captives taken could be sold as slaves in Canada, or sold back to their families for ransom. The English and French also took advantage of the chance to make money during times of war. Many of the captives taken by Benjamin Church and sent back to Boston during his raids east were later sold into slavery. Many of Boston's richest families became even wealthier due to their trading in human lives.

During these conflicts both the colonial governments of France and England began to offer bounties for the scalps of their enemies. As much as one hundred pounds were offered per scalp, turning what would be known as "scalp hunting" into an economy in itself. Groups of New England businessmen, wanting to get in on the action, but not willing to go out and do the work themselves, would finance expeditions in search of scalps, and then they would share in the profits of a successful hunt.

John Lovewell was born on October 14, 1691. As a child growing up on the frontier he and his family witnessed firsthand the effects of French and Indian raids among the English settlements. As he grew John would become a farmer, but also was an experienced woodsman and hunter, using these skills to provide for his family. He was quite successful and by 1724 he and his wife and children lived on a two hundred acre farm in Dunstable, New Hampshire, and also owned and operated a sawmill along the Nashua River.

As was the case with most men who lived in these early settlements, John was a member of the local militia, but his military experience would take a distinct turn in September of 1724. Two local men were in the area tapping pine trees to make turpentine. They asked John if they could sleep in his sawmill for the night, which John granted. Going the next morning to his sawmill to visit the men, he could not find them, so he next went to the pine grove where they had been working, and found evidence that the men had been abducted by Indians. John called out the alarm and nine men from the local militia turned out and began to follow the enemy by their tracks. This party would prove to be a large force of Indians led by French officers. The natives thinking that if they were discovered, the English would certainly pursue them, and so the raiders set an ambush along their trail as they retreated back towards Canada. The nine English militiamen fell right into the trap. Only one of the nine would live through the ambush. He turned and ran into the brush and was able to outdistance two natives who chased after him causing them to give up their pursuit. The two men captured at the pine grove would be marched all the way to Montreal where they were finally able to arrange for their release if they agreed to build a saw-mill for the French in exchange.

With winter approaching and the hard work on his farm done for the year, Lovewell, his brother-in-law Josiah, and their friend Jonathan Robbins began to think of putting together an expedition in search of Indian scalps, the lure of one hundred pounds per head being too much to pass up. They went to the General Court in Boston to request permission and funding for the mission, offering to assemble a party of fifty men, who would provide their own arms, clothing, and blankets, in exchange for a per day wage of two shillings and six pence per man, as well as the rights to any goods taken and of course, the one hundred pound bounty per scalp.

The court agreed to fund the expedition and commissioned Lovewell as Captain, and Josiah and Jonathan as his Lieutenants. The officers were only able to enlist thirty men, but they were all good woodsmen. Setting out in the winter cold the party followed the Merrimack River in search of the enemy.

In mid December they came across an Indian wigwam and attacked the inhabitants, killing one native adult and capturing a young boy. Feeling overwhelmed at their success, and their food running low, the men decided to return to Boston with their prizes. The adult native's body was scalped and left to lie in the open. At Boston they appeared before the court with the scalp and the boy in hand, and were rewarded with 200 pounds, being given an extra fifty pounds for their good success. As the men headed towards home they were already counting the money from their next scalp hunt in their heads.

Lovewell's officers began to enlist men for their next expedition. The news of the success of the first scalp hunt, and the lure of easy money to be made, enticed eighty-seven men to enlist for Lovewell's new company of rangers. Setting out on their snowshoes pulling sleds of provisions behind them, the force ranged the wilderness for the next month towards the Saco River in Maine. A large village of Pequawket Indians lived nearby and this was their intended target. As they made their way north they scoured the area for any sign of the enemy, but after a month in the field, they had found not a single native. Provisions, which the men intended to augment with animals they hunted, were running low. The game had been scarce and the party had slim luck in their hunting. It was decided that the men would cast lots to see who would stay with the party, and who would be sent home because the short provisions would no longer support the full company. The men were loath to be sent back, still enticed by the lure of the great rewards they stood to reap, but in the end thirty men who had their names drawn were sent home.

Continuing on, the rest of the party had the good fortune to kill a moose, which much refreshed the men. With their renewed strength they continued on their mission. John Lovewell was turning into a very able and cautious ranger Captain. His men had complete trust in him, and he began to improve upon the tactics previously used by men such as Benjamin Church and his rangers. When the rangers marched they marched spread out in an Indian file as the natives did, but whenever they stopped Lovewell would send a part of his force back to set an ambush along the trail they came in on in case they were being followed. If their numbers were sufficient this rear guard could spring an ambush, or send a man back to warn the main body of rangers about the approach of the enemy if they were too strong to attack. Many times when his men thought they might engage the enemy, Lovewell would have his men strip off their packs and blankets to lighten themselves for battle. John would always leave a small party behind to guard their packs while the rest advanced against their target. Lovewell cautioned his men that when they engaged an enemy force to never fire all of their muskets at once, but rather to fire in volleys, always keeping a certain number of men held in reserve with loaded muskets.

Marching onward the men came upon the tracks of a party of Indians according to this entry in Lovewell's journal which he kept of the scout.

"We traveled 6 miles and came upon the tracks of Indians, and we left 16 men with our packs and the rest pursued the tracks till dark that night and staid there all night, and on the 17th we followed their tracks till about 8 o'clock." We then found where the Indians had lain twenty-four hours before, and having no victuals, returned again to the 16 men we had left our packs with and refreshed ourselves. We all pursued the remaining part of that day and the night." (Kayworth/Potvin, 51)

After several weeks out on this expedition, without seeing any Indians, the party finally had come across some sign of the enemy. Quickly returning to their spot of the night before, the entire group set out to follow the trail left by the Indian party. Suddenly on their march they saw smoke rising in the air in front of them. Sending some scouts forward to check on the source of the smoke, they soon returned and told Lovewell that the Indians were encamped just ahead on a piece of high ground. The Indians had fires started and were preparing a meal. Lovewell determined to wait until dark before he attacked the Indians, so he and his men waited until nightfall without fires that might be seen or smelled and give their presence away. As nightfall neared Lovewell split his men into three groups and had them creep towards the Indian's campsite, surrounding it. There were ten Indians in the enemy party, and they were all asleep beside the fire. A volley from the first group of rangers would be fired at the Indians on Lovewell's signal. This would be followed by another volley from the second group, with the third group holding their fire in reserve. The sleeping natives didn't know what hit them. The first volley killed or wounded a majority of the enemy, with the second killing all of the rest except for one who ran into the woods to escape. One of the rangers' dogs quickly caught up with him and he was killed as well.

The assault was a complete victory. Looking over the goods and weapons that the Indians had with them it was concluded that they were a raiding party because they carried snowshoes, extra moccasins and blankets, and had several fine muskets and plenty of ammunition. The natives were scalped and their goods plundered for anything of value. Now, having met with success on this expedition, the rangers started their journey home. When they made camp that night Lovewell sent men back to check their trail to make sure they weren't being followed. Even though they had been fortunate so far on their expedition, they were still far from home, and could not afford to let their caution down.

On their journey back they passed through many small towns and settlements, where they were treated as returning heroes. The settlers there had long been the victims of French and Indian raiders, and were most pleased that the shoe was now on the other foot. Reaching Boston the men were well rewarded for their efforts. They received one thousand pounds bounty money for the scalps, their daily wages as agreed upon, plus the ten captured muskets of the natives were sold for another seventy pounds. Captain John Lovewell could not wait to begin planning another scalp hunt.

The next expedition was soon put into motion. Captain Lovewell had been authorized by the General Court to raise fifty men at the previously determined per day wages and rewards. It was almost springtime, and the farms of the rangers would soon be a blur of work. The expedition must set out now in order to accomplish their task and return before spring planting began. This time, instead of ranging to the east in search of the enemy, the rangers would march directly towards the Pequawket village. Chief Paugus and his warriors had raided the New England settlements for years, and now the English would attack them right at their homes.

Forty-five men enlisted for the mission, but only a few of the veterans of the second expedition signed up. Perhaps it was fatigue from the last mission when they had been out on the open for so long or maybe it was the fact that the season was so far advanced. Whatever the reason was, this expedition would be conducted with new men, whose mettle as Indian fighters was untested.

The English rangers started out on their journey, traveling light and quick. By the time they had reached the lake at Ossipee, several men had fallen sick and could not continue. Lovewell ordered a small fort to be constructed at the site to provide shelter for the ill men. He and the rest of the party would continue on to their target, and then upon their return they would rendezvous with the sick men for the return home. Supplies were left at the fort to sustain the sick men, and for their own return. Bidding their comrades farewell, Lovewell, and the rest of the men set out to cover the remaining thirty miles to their intended target, the Pequawket village.

The rangers moved more cautiously as they got nearer to the Indian village. Chief Paugus and his warriors were known for their fighting ability, and the village itself was surrounded by a stockade. With their diminished numbers it would be extremely difficult to assault the village, but the men determined to continue on saying.

"We came to see the enemy; we have all along prayed God we might find them; and we had rather trust providence with our lives, yes, die for our country, than try to return without seeing them, if we might, and be called cowards for our pains." (Kayworth/Potvin, 141)

The rangers stopped at Saco pond for the night. They were in enemy territory and did not want to stumble upon the natives unprepared. The next day, knowing the village was close, they stripped off their packs as was their custom before going into battle. The rangers began moving forward when they heard a shot in the distance. Had they been discovered? Cautiously moving forward towards the sound of the shot they saw an Indian coming towards them. He had two muskets with him and was hunting ducks along the pond. The native spied the rangers and quickly shouldered one of the muskets and fired, hitting Captain Lovewell in the stomach. Samuel Whiting was also hit from the spray of the shot the Indian was using to hunt the ducks with. The Indian was shot and killed by Seth Wyman. The rangers looked to their fallen commander, who was badly wounded when the shot punctured his intestines. Captain Lovewell assured his men he could continue in his duties. The Indian was quickly scalped and the men determined to return to where they had left their packs.

Captain Lovewell had made an uncharacteristic mistake when he had ordered his men to leave their packs in preparation for battle; he did not leave a small party of men behind to guard them as he had always done in the past. Perhaps it was because his numbers were so low and he feared weakening his force anymore, or maybe it was just a simple mistake. Whatever the case was, it would mean deadly consequences for Lovewell and his rangers.

Chief Paugus had been out with a raiding party of approximately eighty warriors, having gone towards the English settlements along the coast, but they had been discovered, and decided it was best to return to their village instead of risking any action with the now alert colonists. As they were returning to Pequawket valley they came upon the packs left by Lovewell's men. Quickly determining that an English raiding party was nearby, the warriors set an ambush at the site, knowing the rangers would return to their packs. Dividing his force into two groups,

Paugus laid out his plan of attack. The first party would lie concealed allowing the rangers to pass by them undiscovered. As soon as the rangers passed they were to spring up and attack them from the rear, hopefully sending them running right into the other half of the force concealed near where the rangers had left their packs. The natives knew they outnumbered the rangers by the number of packs that they had found, and felt that if they could get the rangers in between the two groups, it would be easy to surround and overwhelm them.

The approaching rangers walked right into the trap. At the first volley Captain Lovewell and several other rangers fell dead or dying, and many others were wounded. Paugus and his warriors sprang up and ran towards the rangers to finish them off, but instead they got a surprise of their own. The rangers, after the initial assault, had regained their senses and rallied. Falling back towards a pine grove for cover the rangers kept up a constant and deadly fire against the pursuing natives, which killed several. Most of the officers of Lovewell's command had been killed or wounded, so Seth Wyman took control of the remaining rangers, who continued to fire at the enemy from the cover of the trees.

The natives tried to surround the rangers' position, but seeing this, Wyman ordered a fighting withdrawal back towards Saco Pond, taking up a position where a natural barrier of earth and rocks had formed. The fire from the natives was intense and Wyman soon realized he and the rest of the rangers could not hold out much longer. A better defensive position must be found or they would be simply overrun by the superior numbers of the enemy.

A sandy peninsula lay directly behind the rangers' position. Several large pine trees had fallen down beside a small swampy area. If the rangers could reach those pines, they could use them for cover while the swamp protected one of their flanks. Having lost so many of their men, this might be their only chance to survive. Wyman and the remaining rangers began another fighting retreat successfully reaching the protection of the fallen pines.

Paugus and his warriors for some unknown reason continued to assault the ranger position when they could have surrounded them and waited for the rangers, who were without their packs, to either run out of ammunition or water. The battle raged on for several hours with the rangers rationing their ammunition and making their shots count. The natives, dispirited that they had not been able to overwhelm the rangers, fell back to the pine grove to discuss what to do next.

Seth Wyman, with the firing from the natives dying down, crept forward to the pines to see what the natives were up too. Finding them in the midst of a powwow, he fired at and killed one of the natives, who turned out to be their Shaman, or spiritual leader. Paugus and his warriors, enraged at their loss, continued the battle with renewed force. During the ensuing fight, Chief Paugus was killed by one of the rangers, and soon, with darkness approaching, the firing from the natives suddenly stopped.

As it got darker Wyman sent some of his rangers out in search of the enemy, who found they had left the battlefield. The Indians, after suffering many casualties, including their Shaman and Chief, had decided to break off the battle and return to their village.

Wyman gathered his remaining men together and assessed the situation. Many were badly wounded, but could travel. Three men were mortally wounded; including Jonathan Robbins, veteran of Lovewell's other two expeditions. With courage these men agreed to be left behind, knowing that if they lived to see the morning, the natives would be back to finish them off. Having no other choice Wyman and the others began the march back to the fort at Ossipee where they had left their comrades and supplies for the return trip, supplies vitally needed by the wounded and hungry rangers. Traveling only a few miles four of the wounded men could not go on any farther. The rest of the rangers were either too exhausted or badly wounded themselves to carry the men. Begging the rest of the party to go on to the fort and bring back the supplies and men waiting there, the four lay down and waited for relief or death, whichever would claim them. Reluctantly the rangers continued on.

Fate on this day would once again not be on their side. During the initial native volley at the knapsack ambush site, one of the rangers, Benjamin Hassell, seeing Captain Lovewell fall and the natives rushing in for the kill, had turned and ran for his life towards the lake at Ossipee. Arriving at the fort Hassell reported that all of Lovewell's command had been ambushed and destroyed to the man. Many of the rangers wanted to wait at the fort to see if any survivors straggled in, but fear soon got the best of them. Leaving a sack of bread and pork inside the fort with a note telling any survivors their intentions, the rangers took off for home.

Wyman and the survivors of the battle finally reached the fort only to find it deserted. The pork and bread left behind did much to revive their strength, but without fresh any men to help to carry in the wounded rangers they had left behind, they too decided to march for home, leaving some of the pork and bread behind in the off chance anyone else might make it to the fort. Along their march they had lost one man who became separated from the party, but came upon another man wounded early in the ambush. Thinking he was dying, he had tried to make it back to the fort. Wyman and fifteen other rangers managed to make it home after a four day struggle through the wilderness. Two of the four wounded rangers left behind would eventually make it back as well, at times literally dragging themselves towards home.

The Governor would send out a force of men to enact revenge on the Pequawket town, but when they arrived the village had been abandoned. Fearing just such a reprisal, the natives had fled the area. Finding the site of the battle the soldiers could do nothing but bury the remains of the rangers. Lovewell's Rangers had met with a stinging defeat, but the use of rangers fighting in an irregular fashion against the French and Indians would continue.

Dummer's War or "Lovewell's War" as it would also become known, would basically end after the action at Saco Pond. Tensions between the Natives and the English would die down somewhat, but the fire for battle still smoldered inside the hearts of the two enemies.

The Author is dressed in civilian clothes such as those worn by John Lovewell's rangers. He is armed with a fowling piece, and has his knapsack and bedroll ready for the march against the enemy.

John Gorham's Rangers

Groups of rangers would continue to be used by the English colonies to help protect their frontiers for the next two decades after Lovewell's battle at Saco Pond. French and Indian raids would still strike fear into the hearts of English settlers, but officially, France and England were at peace with one another. That was due to change.

War would come again to North America in the form of "King George's War" in 1744. The New England frontier was again the target of raiders from Canada and Natives from the east. Another native son of Massachusetts, John Gorham, would take up the mantle of "Ranger."

John Gorham was born in Barnstable, Massachusetts in 1709. In his younger years he was employed as a hand working aboard some of the trading ships that plied the New England costal waters. John came from a family with a long military background, and he and several of his brothers would follow suit. John Gorham the 1st fought in King Philip's War, John the 2nd was a member of Benjamin Church's Rangers and fought in both King Philip's and King William's Wars. His father, John III would enlist and fight in King George's War.

At the end of Queen Anne's War, Great Britain gained the mainland of Acadia through the Treaty of Utrecht, which they promptly renamed Nova Scotia. For years Britain held on to a tenuous foothold there trying to establish English settlements, but their success was minimized by conflicts with the area natives and the French inhabitants, who were not overwhelmed to be considered British subjects. The British garrison at Annapolis Royal was attacked by French troops and their allies, the Mi'kmaq Indians. The garrison commander sent word to Governor Shirley of Massachusetts pleading for help.

Governor Shirley responded by sending Captain Edward Tyng and some provincial troops to their relief, including John Gorham in command of a mixed company of English rangers and fifty Mohawk Indians from New York. This would be the birth of "Gorham's Rangers."

Arriving at Annapolis Royal, Gorham and his ranger company promptly went to work, but not in the direct defense of the post, at least not in a traditional manner. Instead the rangers took to the field to strike at the enemy and force them to lift the siege. The rangers attacked a group of Indians in the area killing several and causing the rest to flee.

The tactics used by Gorham and his rangers included trying to inflict as much terror on the local natives as possible. A French priest, Father Maillard, would later claim that some of Gorham's first victims were pregnant women and small children. Another factor in these offensive strikes against the natives was an economic one. Governor Shirley in his proclamation authorizing the relief force of Massachusetts troops included the following directives.

"That there be granted to be paid out of the public treasury to any company, party or person ...who shall voluntarily, and at their own cost,...go out and kill a male Indian of the age of 12 or upwards...for as long as the war shall continue, ... and produce his scalp in evidence of his death, the sum of 100 pounds in bills of credit of the Province of New England; and 105 pounds for any male ... who shall be taken captive; ... 50 pounds ... for women, and for children under the age of twelve ... killed in fight; ... and 55 ... (for those) taken prisoner, together with plunder."

This was vicious and bloody work, but the rangers fell to it with determination, this was war, and it didn't give any consideration for age or gender. The irregular tactics used by the rangers had the desired effect and British garrison soon gained a little breathing room. Gorham and his men would continue their scouting missions into the wilderness of Nova Scotia doing what damage they could to the enemy's food supplies and homes. Gorham's Rangers would earn a well deserved reputation for their fighting abilities.

Leaving the situation at Annapolis Royal in much better shape than when he and his men had arrived, Gorham returned to Boston where plans were being formed for an expedition against the French Fortress at Louisbourg. Governor Shirley and Governor Benning Wentworth of New Hampshire were enlisting men for the campaign which would be made up entirely of North American colonists, mainly from the New England colonies. The planned assault was in response to a French attack on the British fort on Grassy Island, which protected the fishing port of Canso. Fishing rights to the Grand Banks had long been a point of conflict between France and England, who both sought to control this vital economic source of trade in the New World. The French force that attacked the port and burned the fort to the ground had sailed from Louisbourg.

The fortress at Louisbourg, which was basically a fortified town, had been established in 1719 to protect French fishing rights in the area, and also to guard the passageway into the St. Lawrence River by which an enemy could travel to invade the interior of Canada. The massive fortifications would take years and large sums of French funds to complete, but the benefits of the location more than made up for the expense. The salt water port in the harbor of Louisbourg provided a safe haven for French ships to anchor in water free of ice during the winter months. French inhabitants from Acadia migrated to the area when the British gained control of their homes, and this influx of new settlers, coupled with the port turning into a prime site from which to import and export goods to and from France, soon turned the town into a small city.

The assault against the fortress would be a combined effort of provincial land troops with support from the Royal Navy. Louisbourg had strong batteries and defenses covering the approach from the Atlantic side of the city, but the English forces felt that the fortress was vulnerable from the land if a proper European style siege with approach trenches and artillery batteries were used against the city.

According to plan the English forces set sail for Louisbourg in March of 1745 in a vast armada of ships under the command of William Pepperell. The 7th Massachusetts Provincial Regiment, commanded by Colonel John Gorham III, made up some of the 4200 men and sailors assigned to the expedition. His son John, late of the rangers in Nova Scotia, was convinced to accept a commission as Lt. Colonel of the regiment. While at Boston preparing for the expedition Lt. Colonel Gorham was been in charge of securing whale boats for landing the army.

When the army arrived at Louisbourg they first attacked any French fishing vessels and smaller villages in the area forcing the inhabitants to flee to the protection of the fort. The English troops then began to land their forces at Garabus bay led by Lt. Colonel Gorham, while the fort's defenders were kept busy with a continuous bombardment by cannon from the Royal Navy. Cannon landed with the troops were hauled on sleds to the landward approaches of Louisbourg, and once batteries were established, they too began to hurl shot and shell at the fortress.

The garrison inside the fortress was ill prepared to withstand a siege. France, embroiled in the war at home, neglected to send adequate aid to the garrison and food and munitions were dangerously low even at the beginning of the siege. Nevertheless the French forces were able to hold out for six weeks against their attackers, but finally after such a long bombardment, they were forced to capitulate in June of 1745.

The English forces made what repairs they could to the damaged fortress, then leaving a number of troops to garrison the fort over the winter, they sailed back home in triumph. Among those who stayed were Colonel and Lt. Colonel Gorham. Like many a soldier forced to spend a long, cold winter in garrison, where sickness could run through a body of men like a cannon shot, Colonel Gorham took ill and died at Louisbourg. His son John, being second in command of the regiment, assumed leadership of the 7th Massachusetts upon his father's death in February of 1746. Gorham would continue in this position until April when he returned to Boston after being relieved by British regular troops sent to garrison the fortress.

John had returned home for just a short while before he was again commissioned as Captain of a company of rangers with his brother Joseph as his Lieutenant, and assembling their men, returned to Nova Scotia. While there he and his rangers established a series of blockhouses at certain points over the territory the company ranged to better defend the frontier, and to strengthen the defensive structure of the province. This series of fortifications would help to maintain a presence in the area and discourage French and Indian raids.

Since Acadia had been ceded to Great Britain after Queen Anne's War, disputes over the exact boundaries of the province had been numerous between the French and the English. Late in 1746, Captain Gorham and his rangers were assigned to a force of five hundred English, under the command of Arthur Noble, which had been ordered to occupy Grand Pre. The French felt that this was their territory and sent out a large force that marched overland and attacked the English killing their commander and many of his troops. Captain Gorham himself had just left the party to return home for a short stay when the attack occurred.

While there he had lengthy discussions about the British prospects in Nova Scotia with Governor Shirley and was convinced to travel to England in an attempt to further the idea of establishing more English settlements in the area to the home government. Gorham hoped to get in on the bottom of any such enterprises because he had, as would be the case with many provincial commanders during the different wars fought on the continent, become deeply mired in debt due to his service to the Crown.

John and his wife set sail for England and were well received there, even being brought before the King himself. Gorham, while in England, also gained the support of the Duke of Newcastle because of his previous successes in Nova Scotia, and returned to Massachusetts with a Royal Commission as a Captain in the British Army. Returning to Boston he raised a larger company of rangers, near one hundred men, for duty in Nova Scotia.

The Treaty of Aix-la-Chapelle would end King George's War, but Gorham's rangers would still be assigned to Annapolis Royal for the defense of the province. The rangers, instead of living in garrison at the fort, chose to live in huts and other small buildings built outside of the fort. This was something that would become a ranger trademark, perhaps being a sign of their independent status and would mirror the way they waged war, somewhat separated from the regular army. Two Schooners with their Captains and crews were contracted with in Massachusetts to operate in cooperation with Gotham's men. The rangers spent the next several months protecting the frontiers of Nova Scotia from roving bands of French and Indian raiders. Gorham himself led a force against the natives living on the St. John's River to try and intimidate the troublemakers there.

A new English settlement, Halifax, was established and to help provide it with protection, Gorham and his men built Fort Sackville along the Bedford Basin waterway. The rangers' presence was a big help in the success of the settlement. Continuing to range between fortifications in the area prevented the French and Indians from driving back the English as they moved farther and farther across Nova Scotia. In 1749 Gorham would again travel to the St. John's River and this time he was successful in getting a treaty of peace signed. The French however would still instigate Indian attacks on English settlements whenever possible.

John Gorham would leave Halifax in 1751 on another journey to England in an attempt to convince the British Government to make a decisive move against the enemy in Nova Scotia. The French Acadians and the Mi'kmaq Indians were still a threat to English occupation of the area. Gorham was also still trying to gain some relief from Great Britain for debts he had incurred during his service to the Crown. While in London John Gorham would contract smallpox and die at the age of 43. John Gorham and his rangers had helped the fledgling English settlements in Nova Scotia to grow and eventually thrive without the threat of enemy attack. John might be gone, but Gorham's Rangers would live on.

Joseph Gorham's Rangers

Upon the death of his brother John, Joseph Gorham (in some surviving historical documents he spells it Goreham) assumed the command of the rangers as their new Captain. Having served as the company's Lieutenant under John's tutelage, Joseph was the natural choice.

Gorham's Rangers would continue to provide security along the frontier of Nova Scotia before and during the French and Indian War. The rangers remained aggressive in their attacks against any French and Indian raiding parties they encountered, using irregular tactics, and mixed groups of English and natives to fight the enemy on their own terms. The rangers also continued to make use of different styles of boats to quickly move towards a target, and then disembark for an assault by land, much in the manner of today's Marines.

An interesting note about Gorham's rangers in the early 1750's is the mention of a uniform for the corps. Most ranger groups wore their own clothing better suited for use in the woods than the uniform of the regular soldier. In the following advertisement for rangers, which was posted in Boston seeking men to enlist in the corps, clothing was specifically mentioned.

"All Gentlemen Volunteers and Others, that have a mind to serve his Majesty King George the Second, for a limited time, in the Independent Companies of Rangers now in Nova Scotia, may apply to Lieutenant Alexander Callender at Mr. Jonas Leonard's, at the Sign of the Lamb at the South End of Boston, where they shall be kindly entertained, enter into present pay and have good Quarters, and when they join their respective Companies at Halifax, shall be completely clothed in blue Broadcloth, receive arms, Accoutrements, Provisions, and all other Things necessary for a Gentlemen Ranger." (Chartrand, vol. 3, 45)

Border disputes continued between the French and the English in Nova Scotia. Great Britain would send an expedition to the French settlement of Beaubassin (near present day Amherst, Nova Scotia). Seeing that the British intended to land at the town, the Catholic Priest there ordered the town to be burnt, and the inhabitants fled. The British would return in early fall of 1750 and build a stockade fort on the site which was named Fort Lawrence.

In response to the building of Fort Lawrence the French would build Fort Beausejour. This fortification was a very substantial, being built of stone in a star shape with bastions and earthen outer works. Two smaller forts, Gaspareaux, and Menagoueche, were also built to shore up the defenses of what was left of French controlled Acadia.

In the summer of 1755 the British would send an army of Regular troops and New England militia men to lay siege to Fort Beausejour under the command of Lt. Colonel Robert Monckton. The garrisons of the two smaller forts retreated to the main French fortifications to help defend it against the British attack. The French forces held out for almost two weeks, but finally capitulated on June 16, 1755. During the siege Gorham's Rangers scouted the surrounding areas to prevent any parties of French partisans and allied natives from attacking the main body of troops conducting the siege. The British would rename the fortification Fort Cumberland.

After the fall of Fort Beausejour, the British attempted to get the remaining French living in Acadia to swear an oath of allegiance to King George, but most refused, instead choosing to flee into the surrounding wilderness. When these efforts failed the British Army began a wholesale expulsion of the Acadians from the territory. Gorham's Rangers were particularly useful in tracking down groups of the fugitives.

It seems that at this time the rangers were clothed in a different uniform than the "blue broadcloth" mentioned in the 1750 advertisement. The following is a description of Gorham's uniform in 1755.

"They are dressed in grey, cross pocket, with small leather caps or hats, according to a French intelligence report. Grey clothing was probably also worn into 1756, as 'some of the French prize clothing' was used for their uniforms 'since no clothing was sent', and this may also have been done in 1757." (Chartrand, vol. 3, 45)

An advertisement for rangers in 1757 gives us another idea of what the rangers may have worn that year. The ad stated that, "The Irregulars in Nova Scotia are Payed on the Regular Troops are clothed by the Board of Trade and have Leather Caps. Another historical reference from 1757 describes the rangers as having, "powder horns in place of Cartridge Boxes." Other advertisements for ranger recruits in 1757 offered "a good full suit of clothes."

Gorham's Rangers would continue to serve with distinction in Nova Scotia until 1758 when they would become part of the expedition planned against the French at Louisbourg. At the end of King George's War the French fortress was returned to the French as part of the peace negotiations, much to the chagrin of the New England troops who risked their lives during the siege of 1745. The campaign was under the command of General Jeffery Amherst, with General James Wolfe as his second in command. Wolfe at the outset of the campaign would be very critical of the rangers in general, not having any high regard for their usefulness as soldiers. His opinion would soon change. Gorham's Rangers, along with the other ranger companies that were part of the campaign, would take to the woods and surrounding territory of Louisbourg in search of roving bands of French Acadians and natives who were conducting hit and run attacks and ambushes on British troops, especially in the British encampments. These ranger companies were under the command of Major George Scott, who also commanded the British light infantry companies for the duration of the campaign. With the fall of Louisbourg to the British at the end of a long siege, Gorham's Rangers would continue to provide security for the British regular troops assigned to garrison the fortress. They would act as covering parties for woodcutters and other British patrols. They also went out to the many French settlements around Louisbourg administering the Oath of allegiance to King George the Second to the French inhabitants.

In 1759 General Wolfe would be put in command of an expedition against the French at Quebec. With the surrender of Louisbourg the St. Lawrence River had become an open invasion route for the British Army. Wolfe was now a convert to the usefulness of rangers and specifically requested ranger companies as part of his army. The six ranger companies assigned to Wolfe would once again be under Major George Scott's command. During the siege of Quebec, Gorham's Rangers would be sent to the east of the fortified city with the orders to attack the many small French towns and villages in the area, preventing any partisan bands from harassing the main army as they conducted their siege.

While at Quebec all of the ranger companies received a new uniform. An excellent description of the rangers' new clothes is given in the Journals of Captain John Knox of the 46th Regiment, who was present on the Quebec Campaign.

"The rangers have got a new uniform clothing, the ground is of black ratteen or frize, lapelled and cuffed in blue, here follows a description of their dress; a waistcoat with sleeves; a short jacket without sleeves; only armholes and wings to the shoulders (in like manner as the Grenadiers and drummers of the army) white metal buttons, canvas drawers, with a blue skirt or petticoat of stuff, made with a waistband and one button, this open before and does not quite extend to their knees, a pair of leggings of the same color with their coat, which reach up to the middle of the thighs (without flaps) and from the calf of the leg downward they button like spatterdashes; with this active dress they wear blue bonnets, and I think, in great measure resemble our Highlanders." (Chartrand, vol. 3, 45)

Quebec would finally fall after the "Battle on the Plains of Abraham," in which General Wolfe would lose his life. After the Quebec campaign Gorham's Rangers would return to service in Nova Scotia. The next year the British Army arrived before Montreal and forced the surrender of all of Canada.

In 1761 Joseph Gorham would be commissioned a Major in the British Army, and given command of what was listed by the British as the "North American Rangers." It also seems that Gorham's men had adopted yet another uniform at this time. The following description of this new uniform is listed in an advertisement posted about five men from Gorham's rangers who had deserted.

"Deserted from His Majesty's Garrison of Fort Frederick, St John's River...Five following persons belonging to Major Gorham's Company of Rangers...in the uniform of the Company: viz. coats, red turned up with brown, with brown capes [collars] and brown insides [linings], which may be worn either side out; Waistcoats of this brown colour; linen Drawers; leather Jockey Caps with an Oak Leaf or Branch painted on the left side.' Besides their weapons, the Rangers also had 'Powder Horns with small straps' and 'small pouches with straps.'" (Chartrand, vol. 3, 46)

In 1762 Gorham's Rangers would be part of the British expedition against Spanish controlled Havana, Cuba. The extreme heat of the tropics, not to mention the hordes of insects and other animals that the rangers encountered on the expedition, caused a variety of illnesses to run rampant through the ranger companies. Many more men would die of disease on this campaign than in actual combat.

Returning to North America some of Gorham's men would be drafted into the 17th Regiment of Foot and take part in the relief of Fort Detroit during Pontiac's Rebellion in 1763. After their service there Gorham's Rangers would be disbanded.

Joseph Gorham had gotten himself deep in debt during his years of service in the British Army. He would be pursued by his creditors for years seeking payment for those debts. Gorham had extensive land holdings in Nova Scotia, but they were of little help in his plight. In 1776 he would be in command of Fort Cumberland when a force of American sympathizers led by Jonathan Eddy tried to capture the fort and induce the inhabitants of Nova Scotia to join the Americans in their fight for Independence. This small and ill equipped rebellion was soon brought down. In his later years Gorham was appointed Lt. Governor of Newfoundland which helped to ease, but not erase his financial situation. Gorham would be forced to move to France in an effort to escape his creditors in 1783. Joseph Gorham would die there in 1790 leaving behind a proud ranger legacy.

Robert Rogers' Rangers

Most Historians will agree that the use of rangers in the 17th and 18th centuries would hit its zenith in the French and Indian War. Of the different ranger units that operated during the war, none would be more famous than those under the command of Robert Rogers.

Robert Rogers was born in Methuen, Massachusetts on November 7, 1731, the son of Scottish immigrants. At the age of eight Robert's parents would take his siblings and him to a new home in the province of New Hampshire. This homestead was on the very edge of the frontier, and Robert would help his family hack a small farm out of the wilderness. As did many a young lad on the frontier, Robert learned to hunt and supply game for the family table. He would also learn the essential skills needed to sustain ones self in the uncharted forests that surrounded the family farm.

During Roberts' early years he and his family from time to time would have to flee their farm and go to the nearest fortified settlement for safety when French and Indian raiders would conduct their hit and run attacks along the frontier. The Rogers homestead, along with many others situated along the Merrimack River were prime targets for the roving bands of the enemy.

At the age of fourteen Robert would get his chance to help defend the settlements against the raiders. He would enlist with the local militia and serve for the duration of King George's War, mainly with companies of scouts who would scour the territory surrounding their homes in search of any enemy parties in the area. They would also pursue the tracks of any enemy forces discovered to try and reclaim any captives and stolen goods.

At the end of King George's War Robert would try and establish his own fortunes by purchasing a plot of land in Dunbarton in 1753, which he began to clear for farming. The life of a framer must not have been to his liking for that very fall he had rented the farm to a tenant, and was soon enlisted in another militia company hired to protect a group of surveyors plotting a road through the New Hampshire wilderness, which was to be built to help promote settlement up the Connecticut River. This of course did not set well with the French who balked at any attempt by the English to expand their territories.

When war between the French and the English exploded in a small glen in Pennsylvania in 1754 the British colonial governments established regiments of provincial troops to protect their individual colonies. Robert Rogers would enlist in Colonel Joseph Blanchard's New Hampshire Regiment, and would see duty along the Connecticut River to prevent any French and Indian attacks coming into the province from Canada. Robert would serve until his enlistment period was up in the fall of 1754.

In the English colonies if a man could recruit enough men to form a company, usually of fifty men, they would be rewarded with a Captain's commission for that company. Seeking that position Robert would enlist twenty-four men for service in Nova Scotia as part of the Massachusetts Regiment. While continuing to recruit men for his company, Robert was arrested on charges of counterfeiting, an offense punishable by death. Although bound over for trial, the charges would suddenly be dropped, and Rogers was once again a free man.

Instead of continuing to recruit men for the Massachusetts regiment, Rogers soon learned that Governor Wentworth of New Hampshire was again forming a provincial regiment there, so Robert instead enlisted his men in the New Hampshire Regiment. This caused quite a stir with the Massachusetts Government, who had already paid Robert bounty money to recruit his men with, and they were not happy that they would not get the service of his company. Governor Wentworth would not release Robert or any of the men he enlisted, and with the war effort escalating, the matter was dropped.

The need for and usefulness of rangers had become extremely evident by the time of the French and Indian War. Most of the regiments would include at least one company of rangers.

New Hampshire would be no exception. When Joseph Blanchard was appointed Colonel of the New Hampshire troops, Robert Rogers would become Captain of the 1st ranger company in the regiment. Blanchard's men were assigned to the 1755 campaign against Fort St. Frederic overlooking Lake Champlain.

Fort St. Frederic, built by the French in 1734 to protect their settlements in the area, as well as to gain and hold control of the lake, was also a stepping off point for many French and Indian raids into New England. After being supplied for the expeditions at the fort, the raiders could travel towards their intended targets by water, then travel overland to conduct their attacks, and then retreat to their boats and escape back up the lake.

The expedition against Fort St. Frederic, under the command of William Johnson, would never reach their intended target, but instead would defeat the French and Indians in the "Battle of Lake George." Rogers and some of his rangers were off on a scouting mission when the fight occurred, so they did not take part in the battle. Robert's men did however gain the attention of William Johnson during the campaign because of their skill as scouts. Deciding against any further action against the French, the English would build Fort William Henry at the southern end of Lake George to prevent any parties of the enemy from landing there, and then returned home ending the expedition for the year.

A garrison of troops would be left at William Henry over the winter months, and Robert and twenty eight of his rangers volunteered to remain there and continue their scouting missions against the French.

Rogers and his rangers would begin that fall to undertake expeditions into enemy territory in search of prisoners and any other information they could gather about the movements of the French and their allies. It was extremely dangerous to travel so far away from the safety of their home base, especially when the French and Indians would be conducting scouts and raids of their own. It was hard work traveling in the harsh weather of the late winter months, but Rogers and his men would soon prove they were up to the challenge.

When the waterways were still clear of ice Robert and his men would row up the lake close to the areas they intended to patrol, then they would hide their boats and travel overland, hopefully undiscovered, towards the enemy encampments. When the rivers and lakes became impassable with ice, they would don ice skates and glide across the frozen surfaces in search of the enemy, or strap on snowshoes and make their way through the deep snow.

Throughout the winter Rogers and his rangers successfully completed many scouting missions to Fort St. Frederic and Ticonderoga, where the French were beginning to build a new fort. During these missions Robert returned with accurate reports of the number of troops stationed at the enemy's encampments, a map drawn of Fort St. Frederic, and many prisoners who provided information of French plans for their spring campaigns. The rangers also engaged in some minor skirmishes with the enemy which greatly heartened the English settlements. Rogers and his men became the darlings of New England for their daring and bravery. The rangers were taking the war to the enemy, and the British Army noticed.

Governor William Shirley of Massachusetts became temporary Commander in Chief of the British forces in North America upon the death of General Edward Braddock at the "Battle of the Monongahela," during the campaign against Fort Duquesne. Shirley was very impressed with the information Robert Rogers and his men had gathered on their scouting missions into French territory, and being convinced of the effectiveness of companies of rangers for this type of duty, summoned Robert to wait upon him at Boston. While there Shirley informed Robert that he planned to establish a company of rangers, under Robert's command, to serve during the 1756 campaign season. Robert accepted the position and was ordered to recruit a company of fifty men, plus additional officers besides himself as the company Captain. Daily wages were determined for the men, and they were each given ten Spanish dollars from which they were to provide their own clothing, blankets, and arms.

Robert was also given the following instructions as to what he and his rangers were to try and accomplish when out on their scouting missions against the French.

"From time to time, to use my best endeavours to distress the French and their allies, by sacking, burning, and destroying their houses, barns, barracks, canoes, battoes, &c. and by killing their cattle of every kind; and at all times to endeavour to way-lay, attack, and destroy their convoys of provisions by land and water, in any part of the country where I could find them." (Rogers, 14)

Colonial warfare could at times be described as a "war of attrition." Not only were the rangers to seek out and destroy their enemy in direct combat, they could also defeat their enemy by literally starving or freezing them to death. For years the English had waged war on their foes by destroying their fields of corn and other crops. Without adequate food to sustain them through the winter many of the French and Indians would never live to fight another battle against the English. Burning the homes and other dwelling places of your enemy would expose them to harsh weather often bringing on illness and disease which would take its toll on their populations. It came down to simple math, with fewer men to fight the next year's campaigns, the strength of your enemy, and their ability to fight, was greatly diminished.

Following the example set before by Benjamin Church, Governor Shirley sent Rogers six whaleboats for his rangers to use on their scouting missions. The primary area that Rogers and his men were to scout was the Lake George/Lake Champlain corridor. These two lakes were the main water travel routes for any French raiding parties coming down into New York. Fort St. Frederic on Lake Champlain had helped the French to control Lake Champlain for years, and now with the French building another fort to control the portage route between Lake George and Lake Champlain, the French sought to control all travel upon these waterways. This would prevent the English from invading Canada along this route. Rogers and his rangers would make good use of these whaleboats in their expeditions north upon the lakes.

Also during the 1756 campaigns a company of Christianized Mohican Indians, from Stockbridge, Massachusetts would also be raised to act as scouts for the British Army. These natives would be paid on the same scale as the rangers, and would have their own company officers. These Indians at times would fall under Robert Rogers' command.

In May of 1756 the rangers were ordered to make their way to Fort William Henry which would be their home base for their scouting operations. Rogers and his men were ordered to travel up the lake towards the newly named Fort Carillon at Ticonderoga, to see how many French troops were stationed there. Rumors had been flying that the French were assembling a force of French and Canadian troops along with a large number of allied Indians there in anticipation of an invasion of the British forts in New York. It was vital that the rangers find out what the French were up to.

Instead of traveling up Lake George to the portage route and carrying their boats overland to Lake Champlain, the Rangers instead traveled part way up Lake George where they landed their whaleboats. It would be too risky to try and use the portage route if the French were indeed building up their troops at Carillon. Rogers and his men instead carried their boats up the side of the mountain range that separated the two lakes. Laboriously hauling the whaleboats over the mountains allowed the rangers to launch them right into Lake Champlain undiscovered by the French.

Continuing up the lake Rogers and his men would beach their boats during the day and travel only at night. By doing this they were able to slip by Fort Carillon and continue their scout farther up the Lake towards Fort St. Frederic. Once past Carillon they encountered a convoy of French boats hauling provisions between the two forts. The rangers attacked this convoy, where the speed and maneuverability of their whaleboats easily allowed them to overpower the much slower bateaus being used by the French. Rogers and his men destroyed the provisions and took eight prisoners. They quickly rowed back down the lake and decided to hide their whaleboats, returning overland to Fort William Henry where they arrived safely with their captives.

Rogers and his rangers would continue their successful scouting missions deep into French territory for the remainder of 1756, using a combination of travel by water and land in order to confuse the French as to their whereabouts. The French had become very aware of these "flying parties" of British troops penetrating their defenses. They sent out parties of Canadian partisan troops and Indians to try and catch them in the act, but so far Rogers and his men had been successful in eluding these patrols.

In July of 1756 change would come to the British Army in North America. John Campbell, the Earl of Loudoun, arrived upon the continent to relieve Governor Shirley and assume command of his Majesty's troops. Loudoun would follow the example set by Governor Shirley and William Johnson as to the need for rangers to carry on the war effort against the French and Indians. The English had so far been relatively unsuccessful in gaining the aid of many native allies, except for some limited support from the Mohawks, facilitated by their relationship with William Johnson. Loudoun realized without the aid of natives for scouting, rangers would have to be used in their stead. Upon surveying the situation in North America on his arrival there, Loudoun stated that.

"Whoever is Superior in Irregulars has an infinite advantage over the other side; and must greatly weaken, if not totally destroy them before they can get to the Point where they can make their push. There is no carrying on the Service here for without Rangers, for it is by them, we can have Intelligence of what motion the Enemy are making, and by them, that we can secure our Camps and Marches from surprise; from here it appears to me that till we can regain the Indians, which can only be done by beating the enemy, no Army can subsist in this Country without Rangers." (Grenier, 127)

Accordingly Rogers was given permission to raise a second company of rangers, to be commanded by his brother Richard, who was serving as Lieutenant in Robert's own company. Two other ranger companies which had been supplied in Boston commanded by Captains Humphrey Hobbs and Thomas Speakman were brought under Robert's direct command. Robert's company along with Hobbs' men would be stationed at Fort Edward, controlling the southern end of the portage route between there and Fort William Henry to the north, while Richard's and Speakman's would be assigned to Fort William Henry. Loudoun also began plans to augment the rangers in the service of the British Army to eleven hundred men.

It was at this time that Robert and his rangers would make their quarters on an island in the middle of the Hudson River opposite Fort Edward. Much like Gorham's Rangers when they were assigned to Annapolis Royal, the rangers preferred to live in small log huts in an encampment of their own. The duties of the rangers were far different than the often monotonous daily duties of the regular and provincial soldier, and this, coupled with the ranger's distinct independent nature, led them to seek the solace of the island. This Island would soon become known as "Rogers Island."

Rogers and his expanded corps of rangers would continue their scouting missions gathering information about the intentions of the French Army. So far Rogers and his men had been on the giving end of any skirmishes with the enemy, but in January of 1757 it would be the rangers' turn to feel the sting of the French. Robert had been ordered to take a party of rangers and gather what information they could about the situation of the enemy at Fort St. Frederic and Fort Carillon. Traveling overland on snowshoes because of the deep snow, Robert was forced to send several men back who had become lame or frostbit in the frigid weather, which was a common occurrence on these types of patrols. This reduced his force to only seventy-four men. Scouting along the edge of Lake Champlain the rangers noticed the approach of several slays drawn by horses coming at them on the frozen surface of the lake from the direction of Fort Carillon. These slays were part of a provision convoy that had delivered supplies to the fort. Rogers ordered some of his rangers to run ahead of the convoy and block their path, while he and the rest of the men would allow them to pass, and then run out onto the ice trapping the slays between his two parties.

The trap worked according to plan, unfortunately, several of the enemy was able to escape and make their way back to Fort Carillon. Rogers and his men destroyed the captured slays and took several French prisoners, who gave the rangers some bad news. A party of Indians had just arrived at Carillon, and there were numerous Canadian partisan soldiers there, both were well supplied and would be able to march at a minutes warning that the rangers were in the area. Knowing that the men who had escaped their ambush would soon spread the alarm, Rogers and his officers held a council of war to determine how best to proceed in the face of this information.

It was determined that the rangers would follow the path they had marched in on back towards Fort William Henry. This was directly against the established practice of the rangers to never return on the same path you came in on, but it had been raining for several hours, and it was decided it was best to return to their campsite of the day before, where they would rekindle their fires and attempt to dry out their muskets, which had become useless in the rain. This plan was affected without trouble, and the rangers began their march back along their original path spread out in a single, or "Indian file."

It would indeed turn out to be a bad decision to return along this route. The French had been itching to get a crack at the rangers, and when the news came in that the rangers had attacked the provision convoy, and would most likely be trying to make their way back to William Henry, a large force of French and Indians swarmed out of Fort Carillon to try and intercept the rangers. They selected an ambush site and hunkered down to await the rangers approach. Sure enough, the retreating rangers soon came into the view of the hidden French troops.

The rangers had just descended a ridge into a valley and had started up the other side when the enemy, who had formed themselves into a horseshoe formation, fired a deadly volley into the ranger column. The rangers were still in their spread out line of march and were able to flee back up the ridge to a defensive position. The fact that the rangers were marching in this fashion helped them to survive the initial encounter with the French ambush. The rear portion of Rogers' men were still on top of the ridge when the attack occurred, so they were able to fire at the French and Indians who had sprung up from the hiding places, and were pursuing the fleeing rangers. This stopped the enemy's pursuit which allowed the rangers to regroup, forming themselves into a circle on top of the ridge with a reserve party of rangers held to the rear.

From this position on the ridge the rangers were able to hold off repeated assaults by the French who kept trying to overwhelm the rangers on top of the ridge. The rangers had lost several men killed, and many more wounded, but they were able to maintain their position until dark, when it was decided that they should try to escape under the cover of darkness, each man taking his own path to safety. The rangers were dangerously low on ammunition from withstanding the repeat enemy assaults, and the enemy was sure to be reinforced by the morning.

Rogers, who had been wounded in the head and wrist during the battle, along with the remainder of his party were able to escape in the darkness, eventually making their way back to Fort William Henry. Several wounded rangers who had been left behind were killed the next morning by the French and Indians angered that they were not able to destroy the ranger party. A ranger private, who had been wounded severely and left behind, was captured the next morning and would later tell of the torture some of the wounded rangers had to bear before they were killed. This engagement with the enemy would be known as the "Battle of La Barbue Creek," or the "First Battle on Snowshoes."

Even with Rogers and his men meeting with defeat for the first time, they had still been able to penetrate deep into enemy territory on numerous occasions, and it would have to be expected that sooner or later they would meet with trouble. The need for rangers was still clearly evident to Lord Loudoun, and his plans for the upcoming campaigns of 1757 would include them.

After the battle Robert's wound in his wrist did not heal properly, so he went to Albany seeking better medical treatment. During his absence his rangers continued their patrols and intelligence gathering scouts.

Lord Loudoun's campaign plans for 1757 were based on an assault against the French fortress at Louisbourg. Robert, whose wounds had healed and was once again well after contracting smallpox, was to accompany the expedition with three of his ranger companies. His Brother Richard with his company was to remain at Fort William Henry and continue in their defense of the frontier, while the main army was on its way to Louisbourg. Arriving at Halifax, Nova Scotia in preparation before making their final voyage towards Louisbourg, Loudoun was informed of a strong French fleet of warships guarding the French fortress. Faced with such a strong and alert enemy, the campaign was aborted.

The French took advantage of the absence of the main British army to lay siege to Fort William Henry. Richard Rogers had died from smallpox a short time before the French troops appeared before the fort, but his company would take part in the defense of the fort, acting at times as couriers sent for help to Fort Edward. Unable to hold out against the superior French forces the troops there were forced to surrender after a week long siege.

Robert and his three companies of Rangers returned from Nova Scotia and resumed their scouting duties. With the loss of William Henry the need for intelligence of the movements of the French was even more critical, and even though the rangers had proved their worth in the early years of the war, many officers in the British Army felt that the rangers were worthless, undisciplined ruffians who had no place on the field of battle. General Abercromby, second in command of the British Army felt that the rangers were "unfit for service," and later in correspondence with Lord Loudoun would express his concern at increasing the number of rangers.

"I hope it was not proposed to increase them to 1,000 men; they seem already numerous enough to govern" (Grenier, 131).

Nevertheless, it was still very apparent that the army could not conduct their operations in North America without the aid of rangers. George Augustus, Lord Viscount Howe, a very well liked and competent officer in the British Army, was a strong proponent of the use and development of irregular troops. When Howe came to America in 1757 he instantly became intrigued with the rangers, and accompanied them on a scouting mission to learn their ways of "marching, ambushing, retreating, &c. Howe was very impressed with Robert Rogers and his corps of rangers. Howe's own regiment, the 55th, would be adapted in their dress and tactics to emulate what the rangers were doing.

Even with Lord Howe's favor and influence on their side, many British officers were still not sure of the undisciplined rangers and their usefulness. Most still felt that the rangers could only be effective as a fighting force if they adopted the proper discipline expected of regular troops. The rangers companies were also very expensive to maintain, so the idea of integrating British officers into the ranks of the rangers was promoted. This would solve the problems of discipline in the ranger companies, and if regular British troops could be trained to act and fight as rangers, the numbers of the rangers could be reduced, and therefore, the great expense of maintaining them would be reduced as well.

In order to implement such a plan, Lord Loudoun ordered Robert to train a group of "Gentlemen volunteers" from the British regiments in the art of ranging. A cadet company of fifty-five volunteers was formed under the direct command of Robert Rogers, who began to teach them the fundamentals of his "Ranging discipline." When trained these men would be offered commissions as Ensign's, and would return to their regiments where they would hopefully begin to integrate the rangers methods of "woods fighting" into the regular army.

The cadet company would only last for less than two months before the volunteers were ordered to return to their regiments. The attempt at replacing the rangers companies with trained regulars would never come to fruition during the course of the war, but one thing would be accomplished during this experiment, Rogers was ordered to put down his methods of ranging in writing and submit them to Lord Loudoun. This manual was called "The Methods & Practices of the Rangers" and would later be condensed into "28 Rules for the Ranging Service," which are as follows.

"1. All Rangers are to be subject to the rules and articles of war; to appear at roll- call every evening, on their own parade, equipped, each with a Firelock, sixty rounds of powder and ball, and a hatchet, at which time an officer from each company is to inspect the same, to see they are in order, so as to be ready on any emergency to march at a minute's warning; and before they are dismissed, the necessary guards are to be draughted, and scouts for the next day appointed.

2. Whenever you are ordered out to the enemies forts or frontiers for discoveries, if your number be small, march in a single file, keeping at such a distance from each other as to prevent one shot from killing two men, sending one man, or more, forward, and the like on each side, at the distance of twenty yards from the main body, if the ground you march over will admit of it, to give the signal to the officer of the approach of an enemy, and of their number, &c.

3. If you march over marshes or soft ground, change your position, and march abreast of each other to prevent the enemy from tracking you (as they would do if you marched in a single file) till you get over such ground, and then resume your former order, and march till it is quite dark before you encamp, which do, if possible, on a piece of ground which that may afford your centries the advantage of seeing or hearing the enemy some considerable distance, keeping one half of your whole party awake alternately through the night.

4. Some time before you come to the place you would reconnoitre, make a stand, and send one or two men in whom you can confide, to look out the best ground for making your observations.

5. If you have the good fortune to take any prisoners, keep them separate, till they are examined, and in your return take a different route from that in which you went out, that you may the better discover any party in your rear, and have an opportunity, if their strength be superior to yours, to alter your course, or disperse, as circumstances may require.

6. If you march in a large body of three or four hundred, with a design to attack the enemy, divide your party into three columns, each headed by a proper officer, and let those columns march in single files, the columns to the right and left keeping at twenty yards distance or more from that of the center, if the ground will admit, and let proper guards be kept in the front and rear, and suitable flanking parties at a due distance as before directed, with orders to halt on all eminences, to take a view of the surrounding ground, to prevent your being ambuscaded, and to notify the approach or retreat of the enemy, that proper dispositions may be made for attacking, defending, &c. And if the enemy approach in your front on level ground, form a front of your three columns or main body with the advanced guard, keeping out your flanking parties, as if you were marching under the command of trusty officers, to prevent the enemy from pressing hard on either of your wings, or surrounding you, which is the usual method of the savages, if their number will admit of it, and be careful likewise to support and strengthen your rear-guard.

7. If you are obliged to receive the enemy's fire, fall, or squat down, till it is over; then rise and discharge at them. If their main body is equal to yours, extend yourselves occasionally; but if superior, be careful to support and strengthen your flanking parties, to make them equal to theirs, that if possible you may repulse them to their main body, in which case push upon them with the greatest resolution with equal force in each flank and in the center, observing to keep at a due distance from each other, and advance from tree to tree, with one half of the party before the other ten or twelve yards. If the enemy push upon you, let your front fire and fall down, and then let your rear advance thro' them and do the like, by which time those who before were in front will be ready to discharge again, and repeat the same alternately, as occasion shall require; by this means you will keep up such a constant fire, that the enemy will not be able easily to break your order, or gain your ground.

8. If you oblige the enemy to retreat, be careful, in your pursuit of them, to keep out your flanking parties, and prevent them from gaining eminences, or rising grounds, in which case they would perhaps be able to rally and repulse you in their turn.

9. If you are obliged to retreat, let the front of your whole party fire and fall back, till the rear hath done the same, making for the best ground you can; by this means you will oblige the enemy to pursue you, if they do it at all, in the face of a constant fire.

10. If the enemy is so superior that you are in danger of being surrounded by them, let the whole body disperse, and every one take a different road to the place of rendezvous appointed for that evening, which must every morning be altered and fixed for the evening ensuing, in order to bring the whole party, or as many of them as possible, together, after any separation that may happen in the day; but if you should happen to be actually surrounded, form yourselves into a square, or if in the woods, a circle is best, and, if possible, make a stand till the darkness of the night favours

11. If your rear is attacked, the main body and flankers must face about to the right or left, as occasion shall require, and form themselves to oppose the enemy, as before directed; and the same method must be observed, if attacked in either of your flanks, by which means you will always make a rear of one of your flank-guards.

12. If you determine to rally after a retreat, in order to make a fresh stand against the enemy, by all means endeavour to do it on the most rising ground you come at, which will give you greatly the advantage in point of situation, and enable you to repulse superior numbers.

13. In general, when pushed upon by the enemy, reserve your fire till they approach very near, which will then put them into the greatest surprize and consternation, and give you an opportunity of rushing upon them with your hatchets and cutlasses to the better advantage.

14. When you encamp at night, fix your centries in such a manner as not to be relieved from the main body till morning, profound secrecy and silence being often of the last importance in these cases. Each centry therefore should consist of six men, two of whom must be constantly alert, and when relieved by their fellows, it should be done without noise; and in case those on duty see or hear any thing, which alarms them, they are not to speak, but one of them is silently to retreat, and acquaint the commanding officer thereof, that proper dispositions may be made; and all occasional centries should be fixed in like manner.

15. At the first dawn of day, awake your whole detachment; that being the time when the savages the savages chuse to fall upon their enemies, you should by all means be in readiness to receive them.

16. If the enemy should be discovered by your detachments in the morning, and their numbers are superior to yours, and a victory doubtful, you should not attack them till the evening, as then they will not know your numbers, and if you are repulsed, your retreat will be favoured by the darkness of the night.

17. Before you leave your encampment, send out small parties to scout round it, to see if there be any appearance or track of an enemy that might have been near you during the night.

18. When you stop for refreshment, chuse some spring or rivulet if you can, and dispose your party so as not to be surprised, posting proper guards and centries at a due distance, and let a small party waylay the path you came in, lest the enemy should be pursuing.

19. If, in your return, you have to cross rivers, avoid the usual fords as much as possible, lest the enemy should have discovered, and be there expecting you.

20. If you have to pass by lakes, keep at some distance from the edge of the water, lest, in case of an ambuscade or an attack from the enemy, when in that situation, your retreat should be cut off.

21. If the enemy pursue your rear, take a circle till you come to your own tracks, and there form an ambush to receive them, and give them the first fire.

22. When you return from a scout, and come near our forts, avoid the usual roads, and avenues thereto, lest the enemy should have headed you, and lay in ambush to receive you, when almost exhausted with fatigues.

23. When you pursue any party that has been near our forts or encampments, follow not directly in their tracks, lest they should be discovered by their rear guards, who, at such a time, would be most alert; but endeavour, by a different route, to head and meet them in some narrow pass, or lay in ambush to receive them when and where they least expect it.

24. If you are to embark in canoes, battoes, or otherwise, by water, chuse the evening for the time of your embarkation, as you will then have the whole night before you, to pass undiscovered by any parties of the enemy, on hills, or other places, which command a prospect of the lake or river you are upon.

25. In padling or rowing, give orders that the boat or canoe next the sternmost, wait for her, and the third for the second, and the fourth for the third, and so on, to prevent separation, and that you may be ready to assist each other on any emergency.

26. Appoint one man in each boat to look out for fires, on the adjacent shores, from the numbers and size of which you may form some judgment of the number that kindled them, and whether you are able to attack them or not.

27. If you find the enemy encamped near the banks of a river or lake, which you imagine they will attempt to cross for their security upon being attacked, leave a detachment of your party on the opposite shore to receive them, while, with the remainder, you surprize them, having them between you and the lake or river.

28. If you cannot satisfy yourself as to the enemy's number and strength, from their fire, &c. conceal your boats at some distance, and ascertain their number by a reconnoitering party, when they embark, or march, in the morning, marking the course they steer, &c. when you may pursue, ambush, and attack them, or let them pass, as prudence shall direct you. In general, however, that you may not be discovered by the enemy upon the lakes and rivers at a great distance, it is safest to lay by, with your boats and party concealed all day, without noise or shew; and to pursue your intended route by night; and whether you go by land or water, give out parole and countersigns, in order to know one another in the dark, and likewise appoint a station every man to repair to, in case of any accident that may separate you."

Such in General are the rules to be observed in the ranging service, there are, however, a thousand occurrences and circumstances which may happen, that will make it necessary, in some measure, to depart from them, and put other arts and stratagems in practice; in which cases every man's reason and judgment must be his guide, according to the practical situation and nature of things; and that he may do this to advantage, he should keep in mind a maxim never to be departed from by a commander, viz. to preserve a firmness and presence of mind on every occasion." (Rogers, 55-64)

With the cadet company being disbanded, Rogers was ordered to take a scout towards Fort Carillon in late 1757 to gather intelligence of the enemy's strength there. During this mission Rogers would try a new strategy in their efforts to try and take French prisoners. The rangers spotted a lone French hunter making his way back to the fort. Robert instructed his men to set an ambush to capture him, and when he came close enough, they were to spring out and take him captive, but when they did, they were to make a big show of it, firing off several guns, and generally making as much noise as possible. Rogers hoped to lure a party of the enemy out of the fort in pursuit of the men, who would flee back towards the main body of rangers hidden in ambush. The rangers were successful in taking the hunter prisoner, but could not entice any pursuit from the fort. The rangers instead went about killing a small herd of cattle that was to provide meat for the French troops, as well as burning several piles of wood that had been cut for fuel. The French inside Fort Carillon fired some cannon at the rangers to drive them off, and seeing no more damage they could do on this scout, the rangers returned safely to Fort Edward with their prisoners.

Upon the rangers' return Robert was summoned to Albany to wait upon General Abercromby and Lord Loudoun. Loudoun had thoughts of establishing additional companies of rangers for the 1758 campaigns, and wanted Rogers' recommendations on the matter. In the end, five additional companies were to be raised, four made up of Englishmen, and one of Stockbridge Mohicans. The four English companies were to be assigned to a planned expedition against Louisbourg that summer, and the Stockbridge Company was to be assigned to the Lake George/Lake Champlain front with Rogers and his original companies stationed there now.

Lord Loudoun also gave Robert the following instructions for clothing his men, including the Stockbridge Indians.

"They are likewise to provide themselves with good warm clothing, which must be uniform in every company, and likewise with good warm blankets. And the company of Indians to be dressed in all respects in the true Indian fashion." (Todish/Zaboly, 87)

It was at this time that Rogers made an attempt at a uniform for his rangers. None of these uniforms have survived to show how they were made, or what they looked like, but there is a historical reference from one of the clothiers that Rogers contracted with to make the clothing for his men that gives us clues about the ranger uniforms.

"The close that Rogers had made for his people are chiefly of Green Bath Rug & low priced green cloths with wt. Mettle Buttons, and white Silver lace Hats, cord or looping on their Jackets, all lin'd with Green Serge." (Todish/Zaboly, 304)

Robert also pushed for an advance to the rank of Major at this meeting, even going so far as to threaten to resign his position in the rangers and accept a commission in a provincial regiment. Loudoun was loath to lose Rogers, feeling that the rangers would indeed be worthless without his leadership, but would only promise to consider the matter. Robert, not wanting to push too hard, at least could be satisfied with the increase in his ranger corps, and so he set plans in motion to recruit men for his new companies as well as filling vacancies in the original ones, and set out for Fort Edward.

In March Rogers and a large party of one hundred and eighty three men were sent out to scout the enemy at Ticonderoga. The rangers were extra cautious on this expedition because there was some concern that the French had knowledge of the planned patrol. On the 13th of March Rogers' forward scouts sent back warning of the approach of a party of ninety-six Indians who were traveling upon the frozen surface of nearby Trout Brook. Rogers immediately set his men in ambush along the top of the brook with orders to let the natives pass by until the whole party was covered by the hidden rangers. At the signal of Rogers firing the first shot the rangers let loose a vicious volley into the enemy, which killed several, and caused the rest to flee back along the brook. About half of Rogers' party took off in pursuit of the retreating natives and ran headlong into a large body of French troops coming towards the sound of the ranger attack.

The natives had only been the advance guard of a large force of French and Indians who were out looking for the rangers, having been warned of their presence in the area by some Indian scouts who had discovered their tracks. The pursuing rangers were decimated by a volley of musket fire from the French troops, losing many killed or wounded in the onslaught. Rogers and his men rallied and retreated up the side of a nearby mountain to make a defensive stand. From this point they were able to repulse several attempts to flank their position, but the rangers continued to lose men to the French attacks. The battle raged on for about an hour and a half with the combatants at times being only a few feet from each other. The French and Indians were finally able to penetrate the ranger lines, surrounding a group of men on the ranger right flank under the command of Lieutenant Phillips, forcing him and his party to surrender. No longer able to withstand the French attack, Rogers ordered his men to disperse in the coming darkness and each make their way to a predetermined rally point along Lake George. Some of the French and Indians pursued the fleeing rangers, but most stopped to scalp and plunder the dead, which allowed the survivors of the attack to reach the lake safely. Gathering the survivors together, Rogers returned with his shattered force to where they had hid some of their slays, and loading the wounded upon them, set off for Fort Edward, sending some rangers forward to request help to be sent in their direction.

Rogers would return to Fort Edward with the survivors of the attack, having lost approximately two thirds of his original force killed, wounded, or captured. It would be the costliest battle the rangers would fight in the war. The French felt that they had annihilated the ranger corps, but they would soon learn that they were wrong.

After this near disastrous defeat Robert was summoned to New York to wait upon General Abercromby, who had assumed command of the British forces in North America after Lord Loudoun was recalled to Europe. While at Albany Rogers ran into his old friend, Lord Howe, who lent Rogers money to recruit new rangers for his now depleted corps. General Abercromby was assembling an army to assault Fort Carillon in the summer, with Lord Howe as his second in command. Experiments to replace the rangers with the officers from the cadet company, and the formation of Gage's 80th Regiment of light infantry had failed, so the British Army would again turn to the rangers in search of irregular troops for the campaign.

Rogers was to have the rank of Major with the following commission.

"Whereas as it may be of great use to his Majesty's service in the operations now carrying on for recovering his rights in America, to have a number of men employed in obtaining intelligence of the strength, situation, and motions of the enemy, as well as other services, for which Rangers, or men acquainted with the woods, only are fit; Having the greatest confidence in your loyalty, courage and skill in this kind of service, I do, by virtue of the power and authority to me given by his Majesty, hereby constitute and appoint you to be Major of the Rangers in his Majesty's service, and likewise Captain of a company of said Rangers. You are therefore to take the said Rangers as Major, and the said company as Captain, into your care and charge, and duly exercise and instruct, as well the officers as soldiers thereof, in arms, and to use your best endeavors to keep them in good order and discipline; and I do hereby command them to obey you as their Major and Captain respectively, and you are to follow and observe such orders and directions from time to time as you shall receive from his Majesty, myself, or any other superior officer, according to the rules and discipline of war." (Todish/Zaboly, 113, 114)

Upon his return to Fort Edward Rogers was sent out to scout the intended landing place for Abercromby's invasion of the Ticonderoga peninsula. During this scout Rogers took a plan of the area surrounding the fort, as well as one of Carillon itself. The rangers had rowed up the lake in their whaleboats, and when returning to them, the rangers had a smart skirmish with a large party of the enemy but were able to drive them off long enough to embark upon their boats and make their way back down the lake. On the way back they met up with the advanced elements of the main army under the command of Lord Howe at Half Way Brook, who after receiving the intelligence the rangers had gathered, ordered Rogers to Fort Edward where General Abercromby was stationed with the main body of troops. Abercromby ordered Rogers to assemble all of his rangers for the coming campaign.

Abercromby then marched his 16,000 man army to the south end of Lake George and encamped there while he assembled a flotilla of boats to make his way up the lake towards Fort Carillon. Rogers and his rangers were encamped in advance of the main body and were continuously sent out on scouting parties towards Carillon.

Having assembled the necessary boats, Abercromby ordered the army to embark and set out for the north end of the lake. Rogers and his rangers in their whaleboats would be in the lead on the left side of the flotilla. Upon landing the army Rogers and his rangers were sent out to secure a small mountain near the landing site, which they did, as well as securing some high ground near the location of the French sawmills.

While Rogers and his men were out in front of the army, Lord Howe had advanced to the front with a portion of the army when they ran straight into a force of approximately 350 French and Indians who had been out shadowing the movements of the British Army. In the brief skirmish that followed the French forces were routed, but unfortunately Lord Howe was mortally wounded in the first volley.

With the loss of their second in command, the army fell back to the landing site to regroup. This would turn out to be a major mistake. Major General Montcalm in command at Fort Carillon, had less than 4000 troops to defend the fort with. Montcalm knew he could not withstand a siege, so he instead had begun to build earthen fortifications along the Ticonderoga Peninsula hoping to try and stop the British advance there. Abercromby, by regrouping back at the landing site instead of continuing to advance the army, gave Montcalm and his men extra time to improve their defensive lines.

When the British did continue their advance they came within sight of the breastworks of the French, so General Abercromby sent his engineer along with some rangers to the top of nearby Rattlesnake

Mountain for an assessment of the fortifications. The engineer, Lieutenant Mathew Clark, returned and assured the General that they were not very strong, and could be taken by a direct assault upon the lines. An attempt was made to land some artillery on the La Chute River, but French cannon fire from the fort sank one artillery raft, and drove the others off. If the battery had been able to be established, the British cannon crews could have shelled the French positions from the side and greatly softened them up before the main assault, but it was not meant to be. The French works would have to be taken by direct assault upon the defenses.

Rogers and his rangers were ordered forward. Rogers' advance guard was fired upon by French skirmishers who were outside of the French breastworks. Rogers brought his main body of rangers up and was flanked on his right by the light infantry and on his left by a group of Bateaumen. The rangers and other troops were soon engaged in a smart fight with the enemy. As this battle was raging the English Provincial troops began to form their lines of battle to the rear of the ranger's position. Orders were sent up for the rangers to drive the enemy behind their works in preparation for the main assault. When the main troops came forward, Rogers and his men were to fall down and let them pass through.

For the next several hours the British troops tried time and time again to break through the French lines, but each time they were driven back with huge loses. The French had strewn the area before their breastworks with a dense covering of felled trees with the sharpened branches pointing outward. This abatis would prove to be near impenetrable, slowing the advancing troops and making them ideal targets for the French troops who literally sent a hail of lead into their ranks. Finally General Abercromby called off the assault, and ordered the rangers to cover the retreating army.

The British Army had lost almost 2000 men killed, wounded, or captured during the attack. This still left General Abercromby with a force of 14,000 men against Montcalm's army, who were estimated to have lost 500 men themselves in the attack, but the fight was gone from the General. Abercromby ordered his army back to the landing place where they embarked back aboard their boats and began their retreat back to the southern end of Lake George, and then back to Fort Edward. The assault on Fort Carillon had turned into a dismal failure for the British Army.

Rogers' four companies of rangers sent on the Louisbourg campaign fared much better. General Amherst was successful in his siege of the fortress ending with the surrender of the fort to his army. The rangers had conducted themselves very well in scouting missions in the surrounding area, and in preventing attacks on the main body of troops by roving bands of French and Indians. Robert's brother James was Captain of one of the companies, who were all under the command of Major George Scott. Learning of the fall of Louisbourg, Rogers would treat his men to a barrel of wine in recognition of the.

"Good behavior of the four Companies of Rangers at Louisbourg." (Todish/Zaboly, 147)

After the successful defense of Fort Carillon, the French and Indians, emboldened by their good fortune, stepped up their raids and attacks against the English. Convoys supplying the areas around Fort Edward were a prime target. In order to combat these raids Rogers and his rangers were kept out on an almost daily basis scouting for any sign of the enemy.

In early August of 1758 Robert was ordered to obtain provisions for his men for a long scout toward the South and East Bays of the Wood Creek approach to Lake Champlain. This would be a large force because of the recent enemy activity, and would consist of approximately 700 men, a mixture of regular troops, light infantry, and Connecticut rangers in addition to Rogers' own corps. Information had been obtained that a large force of the enemy was in the area, and the scouts were to try and intercept them. Traveling towards the intended area the party found nothing out of the ordinary until several days into the mission when the party encamped near the ruins of Old Fort Anne. Leaving their camping spot the party was ambushed by a large number of French and Indians under the command of Joseph Marin, one of the best partisan soldiers to come out of Canada during the course of the war. After the initial attack, the French forces pushed forward and pressed the fight against the forward elements of the British troops taking many prisoners, including Major Israel Putnam of the Connecticut Rangers. Rogers, who was marching in the rear of the British formation, hurried his men forward to engage the enemy, and also sent a party of 100 men to try and flank the enemy and take possession of a piece of high ground, which they did with good success. This maneuver allowed the British forces to rally and drive off the French, who scattered and fled into the surrounding woods and swamps. The defeat of the French raiders at the "Battle of Fort Anne" would cause the French to lessen their raiding activity in the coming months.

For the 1759 campaign season General Abercromby would be replaced as Commander in Chief by General Jeffery Amherst. Amherst, after his significant victory at Louisbourg, was the natural choice to replace Abercromby after the disaster at Fort Carillon. In Amherst Robert Rogers would gain his greatest benefactor. General Amherst was immediately impressed with the ranger commander, and would make Rogers and his corps of rangers a big part of the coming campaign season. General Wolfe was given command of an expedition against the French at Quebec, in which elements of Rogers' ranger companies from the Louisbourg campaign in 1758 would be part. Amherst himself would undertake the campaign to reverse last year's defeat of General Abercromby's army by assaulting Fort Carillon and Fort St. Frederic on Lake Champlain.

Rogers recommended that Amherst authorize an additional two companies of rangers, as well as three companies of Indians, but Amherst would only grant the request to raise some Indians, stating that the original ranger companies must be brought up to strength before he could give any thought to authorizing additional companies. In accordance to these orders, officers of the rangers began recruiting in the New England colonies, and as soon as the new men were ready, they were to hasten all men and officers to Fort Edward.

Rogers and his men at Fort Edward continued their scouting missions in the early part of the year, often during bitter weather and deep snow. These missions were part of a concentrated effort by General Amherst to not fall victim to the disaster of the previous year. An emphasis was put on gathering whatever intelligence they could about the enemy on these scouts by taking prisoners. Amherst would not go into this campaign blindly, and Rogers would be his eyes.

In March Rogers was ordered out with a mixed force of rangers and regular troops towards Ticonderoga to take a plan of the area for the campaign. The French, knowing that come spring another assault upon Carillon would be undertaken, were putting their own reconnaissance parties out in the field. A smart skirmish between Rogers' force and one of these French patrols happened while on this scout, but the rangers were able to drive off the enemy and continue their mission successfully.

The rangers would continue to scout the enemy positions up the lakes trying to drive off any parties of the enemy encountered on these patrols. In June Amherst would bring his army to the south end of Lake George to begin his expedition against Fort Carillon. As they did in 1758, the Rangers would be in the front of the army, and were the first to land at the north end of the lake. The rangers drove off any French resistance encountered there and seized control of a bridge left standing that led to the French sawmills, which they captured as well as gaining control of the high ground there. The French resistance was very light, other than being fired upon by cannon from the fort and some minor skirmishing. The breastworks used to such great advantage by the French last year were soon deserted by the enemy who withdrew to Fort Carillon. Amherst sent his troops forward and gained control of these works and began to conduct his siege plans to invest the fort.

During these early stages of the expedition Rogers and his rangers were always in the advance of the army to drive off any enemy bands roving about to see what mischief they could cause. The rangers, being lightly equipped, moved quickly and were soon ordered to make their way to Lake Champlain as near the fort as possible.

The French were under orders to delay the British advance as much as possible, but knowing that they could not resist a siege against the fort, were to blow up the fortress and retreat up the lake to Fort St. Frederic when Amherst started to assemble his artillery batteries. The French had also put a wooden boom across Lake Champlain to prevent any British ships from passing by the fort and getting in a position above them. Amherst ordered Rogers to go out and cut loose the boom, which he and his men set out to do, first waiting until it was dark to take to their whaleboats. While they were cutting it away, they suddenly heard a great explosion from the fort and saw the enemy fleeing up the lake in their boats. Rogers and his men quickly pursued the retreating French troops and were able to force several of them to beach their boats and flee overland to make good their escape

The fort was damaged but not entirely destroyed, so the ever cautious Amherst elected to rebuild the fort to secure the area and his line of march towards Canada. Amherst had kept parties of rangers scouting towards Fort St. Frederic while he prepared to conduct his siege of Carillon to watch for movements of the enemy. While making arrangements for the work on the fort some of these scouts came in with the news that the French had destroyed Fort St. Frederic and then retreated further up Lake Champlain to their fortifications at Isle aux Noix.

General Amherst immediately sent a strong party of 200 rangers forward to take control of the ruins of the fort and hold themselves there in a defensive position until the main army could come up. When the army advanced Amherst could see how strategic the location was, and so he began construction of a large fort to control the area which he named, "His Majesty's Fort at Crown Point."

Instead of pursuing the retreating French, Amherst was content to consolidate his gains thus far. The General had received no information as to the success or failure of General Wolfe at Quebec, and could not risk advancing his army further until he knew what the situation was in Canada.

General Wolfe had successfully made his way along the St. Lawrence River until he and his army arrived before the fortress city of Quebec. The four companies of Rogers' Rangers, under the command of Captains William Stark, James Rogers, Moses Hazen, and Jonathan Brewer went about their duties with distinction, scouring the surrounding territory preventing roving bands of Canadian partisan troops and Indians from causing much harm to the main army. General Wolfe would begin a formal siege of the city, causing great damage in the bombardment from his artillery batteries as well as from his warships, but could not force the French troops to come out of the safety of their walls. General Montcalm in command at Quebec knew that his only hope was to remain inside the fortress fighting a defensive battle. If he could withstand the siege late enough into the season, General Wolfe would be forced to lift the siege.

After weeks of constant bombardment and failed assaults on Quebec, Wolfe was finally able to land some troops and force General Montcalm to meet him in battle outside the city on the Plains of Abraham. Both Wolfe and Montcalm would lose their lives in this epic battle, but the British would prevail eventually forcing the city to surrender. Elements of the four companies of Rogers Rangers would remain at Quebec over the winter in garrison continuing their scouting and other ranger duties. Moses Hazen would gain particular fame for his exploits at Quebec over the winter of 1759-1760.

General Amherst at Crown Point still had received no news of the success of General Wolfe's army, so he sought out volunteers to try and reach the army at Quebec and return with information about the status of the expedition. These men would have to travel overland through enemy territory. It would be a very dangerous mission, but Captain Quinton Kennedy of the 17th Regiment volunteered to try. His true mission would be under the guise of being an emissary traveling to the area native tribes with an offering of peace, and he was then to travel to

Quebec to give a report of his mission to General Wolfe. Of course while there Kennedy would find out the situation of Wolfe's siege, and then return to Amherst with the obtained information.

Captain Kennedy left on his mission with Lt. Hamilton and five native allies, one being Captain Jacobs of the Stockbridge Rangers. While on their journey they were captured by the Abenaki Indians from the village of St. Francis and taken as spies to Canada.

General Amherst would learn of the capture of this party by a letter from Montcalm at Quebec informing him they were now his prisoners. Amherst was enraged at what he considered the capture of soldiers on a mission of peace. His anger would develop into what would become the most famous of the exploits of Rogers Rangers, the St. Francis Raid.

The village of St. Francis had been established by French Catholic Missionaries in an effort to Christianize the Abenaki Indians living in the area, which they did with great success. The village at the time of Rogers' raid was well built with framed houses, several which have been described as being built in the "French Style," a large fortified council house, all surrounding a central Church building for worship.

The Abenaki Indians had long been the scourge of the New England settlements having raided them with an almost impunity for nearly a century. The Jesuit Priests kept the natives worked up against the English, and when combined with muskets and ammunition provided by the French, this made them a particularly vicious enemy.

Rogers himself earlier in the war had promoted a retaliatory raid against the Abenaki, but had been turned down. With the capture of Captain Kennedy and his party, Amherst now felt that a strike against the Abenaki was warranted, and Robert Rogers would be his sword. Secret plans were made for an attack on the Village of St. Francis by a combination land and water expedition in late 1759. Rogers and his men were at Crown Point with the main army when General Amherst gave Robert the following instructions.

"You are this night to set out with the detachment as ordered yesterday, viz. Of 200 men, which you will take under your command, and proceed to Misisquey Bay, from whence you will march , and attack the enemy's settlements on the south side of the river St. Lawrence, in such manner as you will judge most effectual to disgrace the enemy, and for the honor of his Majesty's arms. Remember the barbarities that have been committed by the enemy's Indian scoundrels on every occasion, where they had an opportunity of shewing their infamous cruelties on the King's subjects, which they have done without mercy. Take your revenge, but do not forget that tho' those villains have dastardly and promiscuously murdered the women and children of all ages, it is my order that no women or children be killed or hurt. When you have executed your intended service, you will return with your detachment to camp, or join me wherever the Army may be." (Rogers, RAC, 136)

Amherst's anger is clearly evident in his orders to Rogers, but it is tempered somewhat, perhaps to sooth what future judgments may be made about his reasons for the raid. Whatever the case was, the die was now cast. Rogers began to assemble and equip his men, under total secrecy for fear of the French gaining intelligence of the expedition, for their long journey into Canada.

Rogers and his party left in whaleboats and rowed up Lake Champlain at night in order to escape detection by any enemy scouting parties or French boats on the lake. They made it to their landing spot at Mississquoi Bay where they pulled the whaleboats up on the shore and hid them. Provisions were left for the rangers' use if they made it back to their boats safely. Rogers also ordered two of his native rangers to stay behind and watch the hidden boats from a distance to make sure they were not discovered by the enemy, and if they were, they were to follow after him and report the discovery to him.

Rogers and his men now began the long trip overland towards their target. For days they traveled through swamplands adding to the misery of the long march. Illness and accidents along the way forced Rogers to send several men back when they became unable to continue on the journey. Bad news would come in when the two Indians left to watch the whaleboats suddenly caught up with the men in the swamp. The French had discovered the boats hidden by the bay. A large party of the French was lying in ambush at the boats in case the rangers returned to them, while another party of the enemy was tracking the rangers trying to catch up with them. Most men would upon hearing such news would abort their mission, but not Rogers and his Rangers. They would push on hoping to outdistance their pursuers and still attack St. Francis. With all the difficulties met with on their march Rogers' force was reduced to only 142 men by the time they reached the St. Francis River.

Upon reaching the river Rogers climbed a tree in the evening and spotted the village by their fires. The rangers cautiously moved closer and stationed themselves securely while Rogers and two of his officers crept forward to scout the town. They found the natives there engaged in some sort of a celebration, dancing, or as Rogers would say in his journals, a "high frolic."

Returning from his scout of the town, Rogers drew his men forward and formed them for battle. They would wait for the break of day to attack after the natives had gone to sleep. The rangers stripped off their packs to lighten themselves for battle. Rogers positioned his men to surround the town, and stationed men down by the river by the Abenaki canoes to prevent anyone from escaping upon the river.

At dawn the rangers attacked, and the surprise was complete. There was little resistance from the natives as many were still asleep from their celebration of the night before. Prisoners were brought before Rogers for questioning. The rangers now faced a very real dilemma. They were being pursued by a party of the enemy. They were deep in enemy territory and the countryside would soon be alarmed by the sounds of the ranger attack. They could not return to their boats, so the decision was made to try and march overland towards the Connecticut River to the safety of Fort Number Four. The rangers would have to move quickly if they hoped to outdistance their pursuers. The town of St. Francis was burned completely except for three buildings inside of which some corn was found. The rangers were nearly out of provisions after their long march, and would need this corn for their return. Rogers ordered most of his captives taken in the attack to be released, except for a few he chose to take with them as well as some English prisoners found during the attack. The party quickly assembled and began their march away from the village and the smoke filled skies from the burning buildings.

Estimates of enemy casualties suffered in the attack varied between Rogers' report and those made by the French after the raid. Rogers himself had only lost one native killed and several men wounded in the attack, most of them just slightly. The French of course listed their casualties as much lower than did Rogers. Whatever the true case might be, Rogers and his men had struck a lightning blow against the enemy deep into their own territory. The French and Indians of St. Francis would never again raid the New England countryside without fear of reprisal.

It would take the rangers eight days to reach Lake Memphremagog. What little food they had was long since gone. Rogers divided his men into smaller groups in hopes that they might be better able to hunt game. The strength of the rangers was rapidly disappearing in their starving condition. A small party was sent in a different direction towards Crown Point where they were to direct General Amherst to order supplies and provisions to be sent to the Connecticut River from Fort Number Four so they would be waiting for the rangers when they reached that point.

Rogers force would lose seventeen men to enemy pursuers and another thirty-two would die of starvation on the return home. Arriving at the point where the requested supplies were expected to be, Rogers, and his men found none, only the remnants of a campfire that they could only conclude was left by the relief party sent there with the supplies. Most of Rogers' men could not continue on in their emaciated state. Rogers and three others continued down the Connecticut River on a hand made raft, finally reaching the safety of Fort Number Four where Robert immediately sent men and supplies back up river to aid his men left there. Rogers himself would travel up river a couple of days later to try and bring in as many of his men as possible.

It had been a grueling and costly expedition, by most considered impossible from the start, but Rogers and his men were used to making the impossible possible. Amherst had his revenge, and Robert Rogers and his rangers would reach an almost hero status with the settlers along the New England frontier.

During the 1759 British campaigns the French forts at Ticonderoga, Crown Point, Niagara, and Quebec were either abandoned or captured. The French forces were being steadily pushed further and further back into Canada. With such great success most of the ranger companies were disbanded for the winter months to save expenses. Rogers, having recovered from the St. Francis ordeal, would be stationed at Crown Point with his own company and one other. The rangers kept out scouting patrols during this time in anticipation of the coming 1760 campaign and what many believed would be the final push into Canada and the total defeat of the French there.

In the spring of 1760 Rogers would be ordered to reactivate his disbanded ranger companies for the coming campaign against Montreal. Rogers with six companies would be assigned to General Haviland's army which was to travel up Lake Champlain towards Canada. Two ranger companies would travel with Amherst's own army to Lake Ontario, and from there travel the St. Lawrence River from the south towards Montreal, while the British army under General Murray at Quebec, with Moses Hazen's company of Rogers Rangers, would come from the north. The plan was for the three armies to meet for the siege of the fortified city.

General Haviland's army would face the most resistance. There were still many French fortifications along the Richelieu River to contend with before they reached Canada. The rangers were once again in advance of the army and kept pressure on the retreating French forces. Haviland's army was successful in sweeping any resistance out of the way and soon appeared before Montreal.

Staring down at the three British armies assembled before him, Governor Vaudreuil had no choice but to surrender all of French held Canada to the British.

The war in America was over, but there would be one final honor reserved for Robert Rogers and his rangers. Most of the ranger companies would be disbanded, but Robert was ordered to assemble a party of 200 rangers to travel to the western French outposts and accept their surrender according to the terms given by Governor Vaudreuil at Montreal. Traveling by whaleboat Rogers and his men were able to reach Fort Detroit and accept its surrender. Rogers tried to press on overland to reach Fort Michilimackinac because it was so late in the year that ice on the lakes prevented travel by boat, but Rogers and his party was forced to turn back due to the severity of the weather. A lot can be said about the confidence and esteem General Amherst felt for the Ranger Commander to place such a task in his hands.

In recognition of his service during the war Robert was given a Captain's commission in a South Carolina Independent Regiment of the British Regular Army. Robert married Elizabeth Browne before he left for his new duties in the south. Rogers missed being involved in a campaign to quell an uprising of Cherokee Indians in the south, but elements of his former ranger corps were present during the conflict. The difference in weather between the south and the northern climate that Rogers was used to left him sick and miserable in South Carolina, so he petitioned General Amherst to be allowed to take a commission in a New York Independent Regiment, or to be reassigned back north. He was finally able to sell his commission and purchase one in New York, but this regiment was soon disbanded, leaving Robert as a half pay British officer.

Civilian live did not bring the same success Robert had known in his ranger days. Enormous debts incurred during his service to the Crown left him with creditors hounding him for payment. Requests to be reimbursed for war costs were answered, but not to an amount sufficient to get himself out of debt.

Pontiac's Rebellion in 1763 would bring temporary relief from his money problems when Robert was ordered to raise a company of rangers to assist in lifting the siege of Fort Detroit. Rogers and his men would serve with distinction, especially in the "Battle of Bloody Run," where Robert was instrumental in preventing an ambush by the natives from turning into a total route of a party of British troops who marched out to confront the enemy.

After the native confederation was defeated and peace was established, Rogers would find himself once again a British Officer on half pay. A glimmer of hope would occur when Robert would be appointed Governor of Michilimackinac, but charges of treason, a failing marriage, and continued financial problems would haunt Rogers for the next several years.

With the advent of the Revolutionary War Robert would again find himself in the service of the Crown. Commissioned as a Lt. Colonel, Rogers would first raise a Regiment called the "Queen's Rangers." Rogers' new corps participated in several engagements over the next few months, but Rogers was soon replaced in his command. The Queen's Rangers were not being utilized in their normal role, instead being given duties as infantry troops. It seems that Rogers may have butted heads with the British command, and thus was no longer needed.

Rogers would get another chance when Sir Henry Clinton ordered Robert to raise two Battalions of Rangers for duty in May of 1779. These men would be known as the "King's Rangers." By this time Rogers was but a shell of the former man he once was. Time spent in prison for his debts and excessive drinking had utterly ruined him. The last action Rogers would see in the war was when a ship he was aboard bound for New York was captured by a privateer out of Pennsylvania. Robert Rogers would remain a prisoner of war until the end of the conflict and would set sail for London with the rest of the evacuating British Army.

Robert Rogers would die in London in May of 1795, broken down and penniless. While Rogers may not have enjoyed success later in life, his contributions to the development of Rangers and Special Forces Units in today's modern military establishments remain his legacy to this day. While he may not have been the "Father of the Rangers," he certainly is responsible for their continued place in history.

Dan Reese is dressed and equipped as one of Robert Rogers' Stockbridge Rangers.

James Smith's Rangers

After the British campaigns of 1760 the war in North America between the French and British empires would end, but peace would not be established until 1763 with the Treaty of Paris. It would not take long for conflict to arise once again in America.

General Jeffery Amherst was still overall Commander in Chief on the continent, and would establish policies concerning relations with the Native American tribes which would breed discontent among the Indians. At the end of the French and Indian War the British Army had occupied the various forts long the frontier that were surrendered by the French under the terms agreed upon at Montreal. These forts located in the Great Lakes regions, the Illinois territory, and the Ohio country were right in the middle of the homes and hunting areas of the various native tribes. Whatever agreements were made between the French and English took little notice of this fact, and the subsequent dealings with the natives showed this shortsightedness.

No longer needing their assistance as allies, the treatment of the natives soon was no better than that of slaves. The natives were a source of income through the trade in furs, but were also seen as a hindrance to westward expansion of English territories. The French had always practiced the giving of presents to the native tribes to maintain their loyalties and to exert them to war, but the British, trying to cut expenses in North America after the cost of the recent war, abolished any large scale gift giving to the native tribes. Amherst also forbade the supplying of arms and ammunition to the Indians. This greatly hindered their ability to hunt and provide for their families. The native tribes had become dependant on European trade goods, and without powder and ball to hunt for furs, the tribes were soon suffering for items with which to trade.

A confederation of the various tribes began to secretly plan an uprising against the British fortifications along the frontier. This uprising is known as "Pontiac's Rebellion," or "Pontiac's Conspiracy," because the leader of the Ottawa tribe, Pontiac, was one of the primary instigators of the rebellion.

In reality the conflict was a combined effort between a large number of tribes and leaders, which basically can be broken down into three groups. The first group consisted of the Great Lakes tribes such as the Ottawa, Ojibwa, Potawatomi, and Huron Indians. The second group which operated in the Illinois territory consisted of the Miami, Wea, Kickapoo, and Mascouten tribes. The third group consisted of the Ohio natives, the Delaware, Shawnee, Wyandot, and Mingo Indians.

The attacks would begin with an assault on Fort Detroit in May of 1763, led by a mixed group of natives under Pontiac's leadership. The plans called for the fortifications to be taken by surprise, but an alert garrison at Detroit prevented this from happening. This would not be the case with most of the forts that were attacked.

Fort Sandusky, a small outpost on Lake Erie would be the first to fall, followed quickly by Fort St. Joseph near present day Niles, Michigan. Forts Miami and Ouiatenon in the Indiana territory came next. Fort Michilimackinac at the junction of Lakes Michigan and Huron would fall prey next. The taking of the fort was a complete surprise initiated by a group of natives playing a game of ball, much like lacrosse, outside the fort's gate. By driving the ball through the open gate of the fort, they were able to gain entry where they quickly picked up weapons hidden inside, or took them from some of the native women watching the game, and thus were able to overwhelm the small garrison.

Another series of attacks would occur in mid June in the Ohio territory. Forts Venango, Le Boeuf, and Fort Presque Isle would all fall to the confederation of natives. News of the attacks had reached Fort Pitt as settlers from the Ohio and Pennsylvania frontiers streamed into the fort for safety.

Unable to surprise the garrisons at Detroit and Fort Pitt, the natives attempted to lay siege to these two fortifications. This is something that the natives rarely did, lacking the necessary artillery needed to batter down the walls of a fort, but they kept up a constant fire from small arms directed at the garrison in an attempt to pin them in and prevent the forts from being re-supplied.

Roving bands of Indian raiders took to the countryside of Pennsylvania killing and taking prisoner any settlers that had stayed on their homesteads or could not reach the safety of Fort Pitt. Fort Bedford and Fort Ligonier, also on the Pennsylvania front, were harassed from time to time by these raiders, but never forced to surrender.

In order to combat these raiding parties Pennsylvania would call companies of Rangers into duty upon the frontier. One of these companies would be under the command of Captain James Smith.

James Smith was born on the Pennsylvania frontier in 1737. As with many a young boy on the frontier, what education he received was minimal, but he was able to read and write with some skill. Living on the outskirts of civilization James would also receive an education in the skills and ways of the woodsman, becoming an able hunter and provider for his family's table.

At the age of eighteen James took a job as a woodcutter employed by the Pennsylvania colony to build a road through the wilderness from Fort Loudoun to intersect with the road being built as part of General Braddock's campaign against Fort Duquesne in 1755. During the process of building this road James and another man were sent on horseback to check on a convoy of provisions that was being sent up to the party of woodcutters. While on this journey they were attacked by three Indians who had constructed a blind of cut green bushes in order to ambush anyone traveling along the road. In the attack his friend was killed and scalped, but James, unhurt, was taken prisoner by the natives, two Delaware, and one Canasatauga. One of the natives could speak English and proceeded to interrogate James as to the whereabouts of any more whites, but after finding out none were close by, the natives took their prisoner in tow and started off on foot towards Fort Duquesne at the forks of the Ohio River.

Arriving before the fort after several days travel, James was met with a sight that struck fear deep inside of his heart. Hundreds of native warriors were assembled around the fort in anticipation of the arrival of General Braddock and his army. Smith was made to run the gauntlet. His English speaking captor told him to run as fast as he could between the two lines of warriors, which he did to no avail. A strong blow from the line took him to his knees, and before he could recover his senses, James was beaten into unconsciousness.

Coming too, Smith found himself inside of Fort Duquesne under the care of the French physician there, who washed his wounds with brandy and tended to him as best as he could. When Smith had recovered somewhat he was interrogated by some of the natives who wanted to know the strength of the woodcutting party making the road towards Braddock. Realizing that the natives wanted to attack the road builders before they could reach the main army, James told the truth about how many men were in the party, three hundred, but lied and told the natives that the men were well armed, when in reality, they were not, and could have been easily taken. This information had the intended result, and most likely saved the lives of many of the woodcutters.

A few days later James was well enough to hobble his way around the inside of the fort, where he saw the natives and some French troops filling their shot bags and powder horn from barrels of ammunition set out in the fort. Braddock and his army was very close, and instead of trying to withstand a siege, some French regulars and a large party of the natives were going out to try and ambush the British forces as they crossed the Monongahela River.

This preemptive attack, while not an ambush, (The two forces actually ran into each other in the woods after the army had already crossed the river) had the intended affect. Fighting from behind the cover of the trees, and from a piece of high ground near the battle site, the French and Indians were able to route Braddock's army. The British regulars tried to stand and fight in line formation and were cut to ribbons. Eventually the army turned and fled from the battle. The natives chose to stop and plunder the battlefield instead of pursuing the British, which would have surely resulted in more casualties.

Smith would witness the triumphant return of the French and Indians to the fort laden with items plundered from the battlefield and loaded down with scalps. Later he would see the horrible torture and burning at the stake of several English prisoners taken in the battle. It was a gruesome sight which James would never forget.

With the threat of an English attack now gone the various tribes that had assembled at Fort Duquesne began to filter away back to their villages. James was taken by his native captors to their village near the Muskingum River about twenty miles from the forks of the Ohio River. This village was a mixture of Delaware, Caughnewago, and Mohican Indians. James feared that he would suffer the same fate as did the captives at Fort Duquesne, but to his relief he soon learned that he was to be adopted into the Caughnewago tribe in an elaborate ceremony. His hair was all plucked out except for a small scalp lock, and he was painted and dressed in the native fashion.

James Smith would spend the next five years living with the Indians, improving his skills as a hunter, as well as observing the natives in their manners of dress, woodcraft, and their methods of waging war. Smith at first was even trusted with a musket, but also became skilled in the use of the bow and arrow for hunting. During his captivity Smith would travel over large sections of the Ohio Territory, the Great Lakes, and Canada. Even though he became more assimilated into the native lifestyle as the years crept by, Smith remained steadfast in the hope that one day he might return home.

Eventually his chance to escape would come. James came upon the information of a French ship filled with English prisoners at Montreal who were to be returned in an exchange of prisoners. James was near Montreal at the time and was successful in getting aboard the ship and became a prisoner himself, hoping to be exchanged as well. General Wolfe's Army had the St. Lawrence River blockaded during his assault on Quebec, so instead James would spend the next four months in prison at Montreal. James would finally be exchanged at Crown Point and make his way home in early 1760. His family was overjoyed at his return as they had never been able to determine if he was alive or dead. Smith had spent so much time with the natives that his family remarked about how much he looked the part, even in how he walked.

James Smith would basically begin his life over after returning home, He would marry in early 1763, but his solace was short lived. An Indian rebellion started along the Great Lakes and soon led itself to the Pennsylvania frontier. The violent attacks on the settlements of the colony would lead to the formation of a committee to raise companies of rangers to patrol the countryside and prevent these Indian attacks. James Smith was a natural choice because of his knowledge of the natives and their methods of fighting. James was appointed Captain of a company of rangers and set about getting his men recruited and ready for their coming duties.

James knew that the only way to successfully combat the natives was to fight in their manner, and so his rangers reflected this belief. In fact, when James later in life would write down a record of his experiences with the natives and his later service in the Indian wars, he had this to say about the use of the native way of fighting.

"Why have we not made proficiency in the Indian art of war? Is it because we are too proud to imitate them, even though it should be a means of preserving the lives of many of our citizens." Zaboly, ACR, 21)

Smith also gives the following description of the Indian's discipline and methods of war in the journal.

"I have often heard the British officers call the Indians the undisciplined savages, which is a capital mistake-as they have all the essentials of discipline. They are under good command, and punctual in obeying orders: they can act in concert, and when their officers lay a plan and give orders, they will cheerfully unite in putting all their directions into immediate execution; and by each man observing the motion or movement of his right hand companion, they can communicate the motion from right to left, and march a-breast in concert, and in scattered order, though the line may be more than a mile long, and continue if occasion requires, for a considerable distance, without disorder or confusion. They can perform various necessary manoeuvers, either slowly, or as fast as they can run: they can form a circle, or semi-circle: the circle they make use of, in order to surround their enemy, and the semi-circle, if the enemy has a river on one side of them. They can also form a large hollow square, face out, and take trees: this they do, if their enemies are about surrounding them, to prevent being shot from either side o the tree. When they go into battle they are not loaded or encumbered with many clothes, as they commonly fight naked, save only breech-clout, leggings and mockesons. There is no such thing as corporal punishment used, in order to bring them under such good discipline: degrading is the only chastisement, and they are so unanimous in this, that it eventually answers the purpose. The officers plan, order, and conduct matters until they are brought into action, and then each man is to fight as though he was to gain the battle himself. General orders are commonly given in time of battle, either to advance or retreat, and is done by a shout or a yell, which is well understood, and then they retreat or advance in concert. They are generally well equipped, and exceedingly active in the use of arms." (Smith, 161- 163)

Smith's rangers would dress in the native fashion, wearing the same clothing he had found to serve him so well in the woods during his years of captivity.

"As we enlisted our men, we dressed them uniformly in the Indian manner, with breech-clout, leggins, mockesons, and green shrouds, which we wore in the same manner that the Indians do, and nearly as the Highlanders wear their plaids. In place of hats we wore red handkerchiefs, and painted our faces red and black, like Indian warriors." (Smith, 121)

Captain Smith would train his men in the "Indian Discipline," as he knew British tactics would not serve to combat the roving bands of Indian raiders. James and his rangers would serve with so much success in protecting the Pennsylvania frontier that Smith was offered an

Ensign's commission in the service of King George. The company was called the Pennsylvania Line and participated in the burning of native villages along the Susquehanna River. This was a corn destroying campaign, and many of the native fields were laid waste helping to weaken the native confederation.

Ensign Smith would be offered a promotion to Lieutenant and took part in General Henry Bouquet's campaign against the native tribes in 1764. This campaign would signal the defeat of the native confederacy and bring the tribes to seek terms of peace with Bouquet.

Peace may have been established, but parties of Indian raiders still struck here and there along the Pennsylvania frontier. In order to keep the natives in a weakened condition trade with the tribes was strictly forbidden under proclamation of the King. Nevertheless English traders still penetrated the wilderness to supply the natives with goods, including firearms and ammunition.

In 1765 Smith became aware of a party of English traders out of Philadelphia who were sending a large convoy of trade goods west to supply the natives. This greatly alarmed the countryside knowing that once the natives were once again supplied, their raids would escalate. A group of fifty men met the traders leading seventy packhorses laden with goods and warned them to put their goods into storage until the order forbidding trade with the natives was lifted, but the traders ignored this request and continued on their journey.

James Smith after so much effort by he and his ranger company to secure the frontier was not about to let this happen. He quickly assembled ten of the rangers from his old company and ambushed the traders, driving them off after ordering them to leave the trade goods behind and only take their personal property with them. Smith and his rangers then burnt the trade goods.

In his journals Smith described some of the tactics he and his rangers employed during the ambush of the traders packhorse convoy.

"The next day, as usual, we blackened and painted, and waylaid them near Sidelong Hill. I scattered my men about forty rods along the side of the road and ordered every two to take a tree, and about eight or ten rod between each couple, with orders to keep a reserve fire, one not to fire until his comrade had loaded his gun-by this means we kept up a constant, slow fire, upon them, from front to rear." (Smith, 123)

Smith makes mention of the use of rifles by the natives during his years of captivity. British military tactics of the time period relied on the use of volley's fired from liner formations using smoothbore muskets, but this was slowly beginning to change near the end of the French and Indian War. The ten best marksmen out of a company of British regulars were issued "rifled barrel guns" to maximize their effectiveness on the field. Smith states several times in his journals that he himself was carrying a rifle. A description of the four hundred Virginian troops who accompanied General Bouquet on the Indian campaign of 1764 is an example of the rifle becoming the norm for irregular troops.

"They were all armed with rifles, and excellent marksmen, and dressed alamode de savauges, with painted shirts and fur skin caps stained with paint." (Zaboly, ACR, 63)

The assault on the trader's convoy would cause a rift between Smith and his rangers, now known as the "Black Boys," and the British military authorities. This conflict would continue for years as Smith and his men continued to prevent illegal trading with the natives. James would even be charged with murder later in his life, but was acquitted.

The independent nature of the Americans would lead to war with Britain. Smith and his rangers would engage British troops operating in Pennsylvania, fighting as irregular troops. James would then apply to the assembly in Philadelphia for permission to raise a battalion of riflemen for the American cause. They replied that General Washington was the only authority that could authorize the raising of troops, so the assembly forwarded the following petition to Washington.

"Sir-Application has been made to us by James Smith esq. of Westmoreland, a gentlemen well acquainted with the Indian customs, and their manner of carrying on war, for leave to raise a battalion of marksmen, expert in the use of rifles, and such as are acquainted with the Indian method of fighting, to be dressed entirely in their fashion, for the purpose of annoying and harassing the enemy in their marches and encampments. We think two or three hundred men in that way, might be very useful. Should your excellency be of the same opinion, and direct such a corps to be formed, we will take the proper measures for raising the men on the frontiers of this state, and follow such other directions as your excellency shall give in this matter." (Smith, 145)

Washington did not approve of raising this battalion of white men acting as Indians, but instead offered smith a Major's commission of a rifle battalion already raised. James was not of a high opinion of the Colonel of this battalion of riflemen, so he turned Washington down, instead accepting a Colonel's commission in the Pennsylvania militia ordered to protect the territory's frontiers, which he would do for the rest of the war, including a campaign against the native village at French Creek. In commanding the companies of riflemen of the Pennsylvania battalion, Smith would incorporate native tactics whenever possible to great effect.

James Smith's legacy would be firmly planted in his wise use of the irregular fighting tactics practiced by the Native American tribes. He could not have known it at the time, but his years of Indian captivity, in which he often feared death, would serve him well in his successful military career

Sam Brady's Rangers

During America's War for Independence the British Army initiated raids by their Native American allies upon the frontier settlements in Virginia and Pennsylvania. They would supply the natives with arms, ammunition, clothing, and food at their various posts, such as Fort Detroit, and then the British would send them out to wreak havoc among the colonial settlements.

These raids would continue on after the end of the war. The natives, feeling increased pressure upon their lands by waves of settlers, many with land grants for their service in the war, didn't need much encouragement to strike back. A series of forts constructed during the war to protect the frontiers of the colonies did little to stop the raids. These posts were expensive to maintain and garrison for the fledgling United States, so once again, ranger companies were raised to defend the settlements. One of the most famous from this time period was the rangers under the command of Captain Samuel Brady.

Sam Brady was born in Shippensburg, Pennsylvania in 1756. His father was a veteran of the French and Indian War. They were residing on a homestead along the Susquehanna River when the Revolutionary War broke out and his father John would enlist in the Colonial Army. Sam would follow in his father's footsteps volunteering for service in America's fight for independence. Sam proved to be a good soldier and very early on was offered an officer's commission, but his father intervened saying.

"First let him learn the duties of a soldier, and then he will better know how to act as an officer." (Eckert, 173)

Sam spent the next year learning the ways of a soldier fighting in many of the battles around New England early in the war. His abilities at the Battle of Long Inland earned him a commission as First lieutenant. Brady would participate in the battles at White Plains, Trenton, Princeton, and Brandywine. His father would be badly wounded at Brandywine, and unable to continue to serve because of his wounds, returned home to recover.

Sam continued to fight. He was at the Battle of Germantown and received a battlefield commission as Captain. He fought at Paoli, Pennsylvania where he narrowly escaped being wounded by a bayonet thrust and captured. During this battle British soldiers would massacre defenseless Continental Soldiers.

War on the frontier was intensifying so Sam and his regiment, the 8th Pennsylvania under the command of Colonel Brodhead, were ordered to Fort Pitt to serve under General McIntosh on the western front. While at the fort Sam received bad news from home, his brother James had been killed by a party of Indian raiders while he and some other men were out harvesting crops. His brother had survived his initial wounds, including being scalped. James lasted for several days before succumbing to his injuries. Brady would also lose his father to an Indian raiding party later in his life.

General McIntosh had ordered that two forts be constructed to aid in the defense of the frontier. The 8th Pennsylvania Regiment helped to build Fort McIntosh, established on the Beaver River, and Fort Laurens on the Tuscarawas River in the Ohio country. While the rest of his fellow Pennsylvania soldiers worked on the first fort, Brady was given another task. Sam was offered the command of a small group of men that were to go and seek out a force of Indians that had been attacking some settlements along the Allegheny River, about thirty miles from the fort on the Beaver River.

Sam readily accepted, and assembling seven men and an Indian guide, they set out in search of the enemy. Brady and his men would use a tactic he would come to use many times during his military career they donned native clothing in an effort to gain any advantage they could if they encountered the enemy. During this mission they ambushed an Indian party that outnumbered their own by two to one. Waiting until the enemy was very close the soldiers fired upon the enemy killing four warriors. Sam and his men sprang from their hiding places yelling and screaming in their native garb, including faces painted for war, causing the remaining warriors to scatter and flee.

With the building of Fort Laurens now complete, one hundred and fifty men of the 8th Pennsylvania Regiment, Brady included, were ordered to garrison the fort. The ability to supply this isolated post so far advanced into the Ohio country was a constant struggle. Supply trains were ambushed and destroyed by roving bands of Indians. The soldiers there existed in an almost constant condition of starvation. Brady would often be assigned guard duty for the convoys traveling between Fort McIntosh and Fort Laurens.

Fort Laurens would also suffer repeated Indian attacks. Bands of the enemy would hover around the forests surrounding the fort and kill any soldier caught unaware outside of the fort walls. Woodcutting details would be sent out under guard to provide fuel for cooking and warmth, and these were a prime target for the enemy. The Indians would maintain a heavy firing of muskets at the fort for a few days, and then it would slowly die off in an attempt to get the fort's defenders to think the natives had withdrawn and let down their guard. When this did not work the firing would increase again. Hundreds of Indians continued to hover around the vicinity of the fort harassing the garrison.

Pleas for relief were sent out to Fort McIntosh. The men at Fort Laurens were in desperate need of additional troops and provisions. Food inside the fort was nonexistent except for what Sam Brady and a few other brave souls could provide. Brady often slipped out of the fort under the cover of darkness to hunt what game he could and return with fresh meat to feed the starving garrison.

The natives would maintain the siege of the fort for over a month until a relief party under the command of General McIntosh himself would arrive and lift the siege. Not being able to sufficiently keep Fort Laurens supplied would lead to its being evacuated in 1779. With the loss of this post the numbers of Indian raids increased along the borders of Pennsylvania and Virginia. The thin, stretched out line of forts along the frontier were kept on full alert, but they were too few and far between to stop the Indian raiders. Colonel Brodhead at Fort McIntosh felt he had a solution to the problem and called for Captain Brady. Brodhead offered Sam the command of a body of men with the following instructions.

"I want you to set up a well-organized body of men to be called Rangers, a force established to search out and attack raiding Indian Parties. I want a group of good, experienced men to make regular patrols along the upper Ohio to watch for Indian sign and give warning to the settlements of any approaching danger. When a report is received of Indian attack occurring, especially when captives are taken, these Rangers are to go to the scene immediately, trail the Indian party at top speed and overtake them, the first priority being to get the prisoners back unhurt, the second to destroy the Indian raiders." (Eckert, 197)

In order to carry out these orders Brady would have to assemble a small group of men, lightly equipped and able to move fast. Clothing better suited for use in the woods would become their uniform. Brady himself would become known for the black head scarf he wore instead of a bulky hat that might become entangled in the brush while traveling in the woods after the enemy. Men who were hunters and able to sustain themselves while on the trail were the natural choice.

Brady's initial group of rangers was made up of eight men, himself included. Strict discipline must be adhered too if the men were to have any chance of success. Sam began to train his men in the different tactics they would use against the Indians. Ambush techniques, methods of marching, when, and when not to initiate any action, and other tactics were practiced daily until they could perform them as if they had been doing them for years. A system of hand signals was developed so that the rangers could communicate without any sound that might betray their presence. The men were also trained to reload their weapons while running, a skill that would come in very handy in this line of work.

Their training complete, Brady, and his men began to patrol the areas between Fort McIntosh and Fort Pitt. They were successful in rescuing two young children that had been taken in a raid upon their homestead. Several of the Indian raiders were killed when Brady and his rangers, having followed the trail of the enemy, had surrounded the Indian's camp in the dark and waited until daybreak to launch their attack. The tactic of waiting until morning light gave the rangers an advantage against the much larger native force.

The success of these early patrols soon helped to swell the ranks of Brady's rangers. Men eagerly applied to become part of his force and fight back against the Indian raiders who had brought war to the frontier settlements for years. Colonel Brodhead, who was now in command of the western army after General McIntosh was recalled east, was very pleased with his band of rangers. Brodhead was planning a campaign against the Indian villages along the Allegheny River and ordered Brady and his men to be his advanced guard.

Setting out in advance of the main body of troops Brady and his rangers became aware of an Indian war party coming their way. He ordered his rangers to conceal themselves along each side of the trail, and sent one of his men back to warn Colonel Brodhead of the approaching natives. If all worked out as planned, the war party would pass by Brady's men, who were to remain hidden. They would then hopefully run straight into an ambush set by the main army. At the onset of the attack by Brodhead's men Brady hoped that the Indians would flee back down the trail directly into his rangers, and the enemy would be caught between the two.

Hiding any sign of their presence, Brady and his men took to the brush on each side of the trail. As planned, the natives passed right by the rangers without discovering them. Brodhead's ambush was sprung early, inflicting little damage on the enemy, but sure enough, the natives fled right back down the trail into Brady's waiting rangers. This time the ambush went off without a hitch. Five of the enemy lay dead and the rest scattered and fled into the forest.

Brady and his rangers continued to act as the advance guard of the expedition for the remainder of the campaign with great success. Another tactic used by the rangers on this campaign involved the use of their own native allies. Like many other ranger companies Brady's often included allied Indians as members. It was common for the rangers as they traveled along the banks of the various waterways on their scouting missions to see the enemy approaching in canoes. Brady would send out one of his natives to try and lure the enemy party into the shore under the pretense of being a friend. If they could get the enemy to come close enough the rangers would spring an ambush from their hiding places along the shore. This tactic was something that both the rangers and their enemies would use against each other.

Another way that Brady and his men concealed themselves in ambush was by building natural looking blinds along the waters edge. Using fresh cut bushes and another material found nearby these blinds helped to hide the men as their prey approached the ambush site.

Sam would become known as "The King of Spies" during his service of protecting the frontier. Sam was often sent out with just a very small number of men to spy upon the enemy and gain vitally needed information about the locations of their villages, the number of warriors in the field, and the trails and pathways they were most likely to be using to raid the settlements. During these missions his goal was not to attack the enemy, but to spy on them undetected and return with the gathered information. The areas he spied upon were often unmapped, or if so, these were often unreliable. Brady would often come back with new and accurate maps drawn of the Indian's territory.

One of the most famous of Captain Brady's encounters with the enemy would occur during a scout in search of a large band of the enemy who were raiding along the Beaver River. While Brady normally preferred to operate in smaller groups of rangers, this time he took his whole force, which by now had swelled to around fifty men, because the enemy force was rumored to consist of sixty warriors. Picking up the trail of the natives the rangers tracked them to their campsite. Brady laid out his plans. He selected a natural ambush site along the trail used by the enemy. Posting two thirds of his men at the site, split in half on both sides, Brady and the remainder of his men would approach the enemy and creep up to their encampment in the dark. At first light on his signal they would fire at the enemy, then turn and run back down the trail towards the ambush site, hoping that they would be pursued. The attack was pulled off on the campsite as planned, and Brady and his men took to the trail with the enemy hot on their heels. At the ambush site, Brady and his men, having reloaded on the run, suddenly turned, and fired at their pursuers. The men in ambush fired at the same time from their places of concealment. Not stopping to see the outcome of their volley, the rangers, as preplanned by Brady, all scattered and fled the area. The plan was a complete success except for the fact that one ranger was captured in his flight. That ranger was Sam Brady.

Sam had scattered with his men as planned, each seeking his own path of escape. Coming to a creek Brady began to wade across the waist deep water when on the other bank a party of five Indian hunters appeared. It would have been foolish to try and flee while in the water so Sam was forced to surrender rather than be shot in his tracks.

His captors took Brady to the native encampment he had just attacked. Sam felt that he would be killed after the damage he and his rangers had inflicted upon the enemy there, but instead he was bound and taken to a nearby Mingo village. Captain Brady was considered a great enemy and would be tortured for the killing of so many warriors in the ambush. The next morning he would first be forced to run the gauntlet, two lines of Indians with a variety of weapons to hit him with as he ran between the two rows. The gauntlet was designed to punish, but not kill him. The natives had other tortures in mind for Brady before they wanted him dead.

Knowing what was in store for him, Sam suddenly mad a dash for freedom as he was cut loose to run the gauntlet. He headed straight for the Cuyahoga River with the enemy frantically chasing after him. Sam knew exactly where he was heading for. From other scouting patrols in the area he knew of a place where the river narrowed, and coming up to the spot he ran with all of his might and flung himself towards the opposite bank. Brady reached the other bank and began to scramble up the other side when a musket ball from one of his pursuers torn into his leg. None of the Indians would attempt to leap to the other side, so instead they quickly went towards another crossing place. This gave Sam, although badly bleeding from the gunshot wound, a few precious minutes head start on the enemy. Brady ran as best he could towards a nearby lake where he plunged into the water and hid among some rotten logs. The natives having quickly picked up his trail by the blood he was leaving behind soon came to the spot where Sam had entered the lake. The natives searched in vain for Brady, and believing he must have drowned, left and returned to the village. Waiting in the cold water until he was certain that the enemy had left, Sam emerged from his hiding place and began to make his way home. The Indians had missed a grand opportunity against one of their greatest enemies. Some historians call Brady's leap nothing but folklore, but fact or fiction, Brady did make good his escape and would once again take to the field with his company of rangers.

Brady and his rangers would continue their patrols along the frontier until the end of the Revolutionary War. He and his men did a great service in making the settlements secure from Indian raids during the remainder of the war.

The Treaty of Paris in 1783 brought permanent peace between Great Britain and the United States. In the treaty Britain ceded all of its claims to the Ohio territory, which of course did not take into account the thousands of Native Americans living there. This was still their home, and regardless of any peace treaty they would not simply step aside and let the Americans settle their lands.

Realizing that there would be trouble with the natives the United States would try to negotiate a separate treaty with the Ohio Indians. There were big plans for the Ohio Territory. Land speculators had greedily eyed the Ohio Country for years and kept constant pressure upon the new Government of the United States to resolve the conflicts and open the territory to settlement.

At the present time the Ohio natives had no choice but to sign into treaties of peace with the Americans because they were in no position to wage open war against them. This by no means meant that the raids upon the frontier settlements would stop. In fact they actually seemed to increase. Although they were technically at peace, the British still supplied the natives with the necessary goods to continue their raids. The Shawnee tribe would prove to be a particularly vicious foe.

Captain Brady and his rangers continued their patrols along the frontier much as if the war had never ended, ranging across establish patrol routes in search of any sign of the enemy and pursuing the tracks of any raiders in an attempt to rescue any captives. The rangers enjoyed continued success in their scouts freeing many a prisoner from the enemy.

Conflicts between the natives and the Americans would soon escalate into an all out Indian war. In response, two large scale campaigns were undertaken against the Ohio tribes by the Army of the United States. The first went out under the command of General Harmar with the intention of punishing the natives and destroying their villages. The natives hounded Harmar and his army as they marched, setting up ambushes and hit and run raids that would eventually force the General to end the campaign. He would claim victory because of the few prisoners he took and for burning some villages, but his losses and his casualties told the real story, the campaign was a disaster.

A second campaign was organized under the command of Governor Arthur St. Clair, a veteran of the Revolutionary War. St Clair was to build a series of forts to secure his route as he marched towards his objective, the Indian villages along the Maumee and Auglaize Rivers. Arriving near the headwaters of the Wabash River, St. Clair's army made camp for the night. In the morning they were attacked by a force of confederated Indian tribes who utterly routed the Americans. The natives had won a major victory over the United States Army.

Flush with this latest success, and with the army being driven back, the Indians increased their raiding upon the frontier settlements. Captain Brady and his rangers were constantly on the job. Brady at this time also went on several spying missions deep into enemy territory gathering much needed intelligence of the enemy's whereabouts. On these expeditions Brady would often dress himself in native clothing and enter the Indian villages after dark gathering information while in his disguise, a very daring and dangerous tactic.

With the Indian war escalating, and after the failed campaigns of Harmar and St. Clair, the United States would again try to negotiate a peace treaty with the Ohio tribes, but these efforts would fail. A new campaign to end the war for good was planned under the command of the newly appointed Commander of the Western Army, General Anthony Wayne. Wayne began to rigorously train his troops for the upcoming expedition. Wayne and his "Legion," as the army was called would meet the Indians at the "Battle of Fallen Timbers," (near present day Maumee, Ohio) and soundly defeat them.

Indian raids upon the frontier diminished at a rapid pace after the defeat. What raids occurred were mainly by small parties of natives looking for plunder. Brady and his rangers were able to start to scale back their routine patrols.

Late in 1794, with so much unexpected time on his hands, Sam elected to go on a deer hunt with some friends. During the hunt Brady would slip on some ice at the edge of a stream and knock himself unconscious. Lying there in the frigid water until he came to, Brady soon became very ill. His friends took him home to hopefully recover from his illness.

Many of the Ohio tribes would sign the "Treaty of Greenville" in 1795 giving up half of the Ohio territory to the United States. The natives over the next several years would continue to be pushed back from their lands, finally living on very small portion of the northwest corner of what would become the State of Ohio. The threat of any large scale Indian attacks upon the frontier was gone.

Sam Brady would never fully recover from his illness due to the exposure he suffered on the deer hunt. At times it would seem that he was getting better, but then he would take a turn for the worse. Sam Brady would die on January the 1st, 1799 at the age of forty three. Peace had come to the Ohio River Valley, carried upon the backs of men like Sam Brady and his rangers.

Epilogue

It is pretty easy to see how significant how the use of companies of rangers were in protecting the frontiers of the English colonies during the 17th and 18th centuries. Without the security these brave men provided our nation would have been severely limited in its ability to expand and grow.

Ranging companies would also become vital to the operation of any military campaigns during this time period. The very nature of the North American continent necessitated the use of irregular troops to cope with the vast differences in terrain that handcuffed the use of European military tactics.

Men like Benjamin Church would adapt their ways of making war to combat their enemies, as well as modify their clothing, weapons, and gear used in the war effort. Items more at home in the vast woods and swamps of North America were found to be much more effective than those used on the open battlefields preferred by regular troops. When reading over the pages of this book it becomes very apparent that the various ranger units studied within operated in much the same way, but over the years their tactics would be improved and adapted where necessary to confront changing conditions and situations. Men like Robert Rogers would bring the advantages of ranger tactics into the forefront of military thinking, and the British Army would soon begin to adapt their own military organization to fit this need. Special Forces units and Light Infantry divisions are now the norm in most every army in the world.

Another reoccurring theme is the adaptation of tactics used by the Native American tribes into the ranging companies, even to the point of using mixed companies of English troops and Indians operating together as one. In the French and Indian War natives would be organized in ranger companies of their own, with their own officers and a pay scale that matched that of the English troops.

Of course this would be a double edged sword for the Native Americans, who would see their own methods of war used against them to drive them from their traditional homes and hunting areas.

Today's modern military forces face many challenges throughout the world, and ranger companies continue the fight for our freedoms, so the next time you and your family enjoy an outing on a sunny day and then return safely to your home, remember the brave men who came before us and helped to provide the safety and security we enjoy today.

Always remember

Rangers Lead the Way

Bibliography

Books:

Anderson, Fred. *Crucible of War: The Seven Years' War and the Fate of Empire in British North America 1754-1766.* New York: Alfred A. Knopf, 2000.

Anderson, Fred. *The War That Made America, A Short History of the French and Indian War.* New York: the Penguin Group, 2005.

Benn, Carl and Marston, Daniel. *Liberty or Death, Wars That Forged A Nation.* Great Britain: Osprey Publishing Ltd. 2006.

Bellico, Russell P. *Sails and Steam in the Mountains: A Maritime and Military History of Lake George and Lake Champlain.* Fleischmanns, NY: Purple Mountain Press, Revised edition, 2001.

Bearor, Bob. *The Battle on Snowshoes.* Westminster, Maryland: Heritage Books Inc. 2005.

Brumwell, Stephen. *White Devil, A True Story of War, Savagery, and Vengeance in Colonial America.* Great Britain: De Capo Press, 2004

Cave, Alfred A. *The French and Indian War.* West Port, Connecticut: Greenwood Press 2004

Chamberlain, John. *The Indian Fighter at Pigwacket.* Weymouth and Braintree Publishing, 1898.

Chartrand, Rene. *Colonial American Troops 1610-1774 Volume 1.* Great Britain: Osprey Publishing Ltd. 2002

Chartrand, Rene. *Colonial American Troops 1610-1774 Volume 2.* Great Britain: Osprey Publishing Ltd. 2002.

Chartrand, Rene. *Colonial American Troops 1610-1774 Volume 3.* Great Britain: Osprey Publishing Ltd. 2003.

Church, Thomas, and Drake, Samuel. *The History of King Philips War: Also of Expeditions Against the French and Indians in the Eastern Parts of New England, In the Years 1689, 1690, 1692, 1696 And 1704.* Massachusetts: Howe and Norton Printers, 1825. Reprinted by Kessinger Publishing.

Cuneo, John R. *Robert Rogers of the Rangers.* Ticonderoga, NY: Fort Ticonderoga Museum, 1988.

Delisle, Steve. *The Equipment of New France Militia 1740-1760.* Maryland: Kebeca Liber Ata Co. 1998

Eckert, Allan W. *That Dark And Bloody River, Chronicles of the Ohio River Valley.* New York: Bantam Books, 1995.

Fitzpatrick, Alan. *Wilderness War On The Ohio.* West Virginia: Fort Henry Publications, 2003.

Fowler, William M. Jr. *Empires at War, The French and Indian War and the Struggle for North America, 1754-1763.* New York: Walker & Company 2005.

Gallup, Andrew and Shaffer, Donald. *La Marine, The French Colonial Soldier in Canada 1745-1761.* Maryland: Heritage Books Inc. 1992.

Gallup, Andrew. *Memoir of a French and Indian War Soldier, "Jolicoeur" Charles Bonin.* Maryland: Heritage Books Inc. 1993

Grenier, John. *The First Way of War, American War Making on the Frontier.* New York: Cambridge University Press 2005.

Hall, Dennis Jay. *The Journals of Sir William Johnson's Scouts, 1755 & 1756.* Panton, VT: Essence of Vermont, 1999.

Hill, William H. *Old Fort Edward.* New York, Privately Printed. Reprinted Massachusetts: Higginson Book Company

Kayworth Alfred E. and Potvin, Raymond G. *The Scalp Hunters: Abenaki Ambush at Lovewell Pond, 1725.* Wellesley, MA: Branden Books, a Division of Branden Publishing Company, 2002.

Kemmer, Brenton C. *Redcoats, Yankees, and Allies: A History of the Uniforms, Clothing, and Gear of the British Army in the Lake George-Lake Champlain Corridor, 1755-1760.* Bowie, MD: Heritage Books, Inc., 1998.

Kidder, Frederick. *Expeditions of Captain John Lovewell.* Boston: Bartlett and Halliday, 1865.

Knox, John, edited by Arthur G. Doughty. *An Historical Journal of the Campaigns in North America for the Years 1757, 1758, 1759, and 1760.* Published in three volumes. Toronto, Canada: The Champlain Society, 1914.

Knox, Captain John, edited and introduced by Brian Connell. *The Siege of Quebec and Other Campaigns in North America, 1757-1760.* London: The Folio Society, 1976.

Loescher, Burt Garfield. *The History of Rogers' Rangers: Volume I, The Beginnings.* Facsimile Reprint. Bowie, MD: Heritage Books, Inc., 2001

Loescher, Burt Garfield. *The History of Rogers' Rangers: Volume II, Genesis: Rogers' Rangers–The First Green Berets. The Corps and the Revivals: April 6, 1758-December 24, 1783.* Facsimile reprint with additional illustrations. Bowie, MD: Heritage Books, Inc., 2000.

Loescher, Burt Garfield. *The History of Rogers Ranger: Volume 3, Officers and Non Commissioned Officers.* Bowie, Maryland: Heritage Books Inc. 2001.

Loescher, Burt Garfield. *The History of Rogers' Rangers: Volume 4, The St. Francis Raid.* Bowie. MD: Heritage Books, Inc., 2002.

Marrin, Albert. *Struggle for a Continent: The French and Indian Wars, 1690-1760.* New York: Macmillan Publishing Company, Collier Macmillan Canada, Inc., 1987.

Marston, Daniel. *The French and Indian War 1754-1760.* Great Britain: Osprey Publishing Limited 2002.

Mays, Edith. *Amherst Papers, 1756-1763, The Southern Sector: Dispatches from South Carolina, Virginia and His Majesty's Superintendent of Indian Affairs.* Maryland: Heritage Books Inc.

McCulloch, Ian M. and Todish, Timothy J. *British Light Infantryman of the Seven Years War. North America 1757-63.* Osprey Publishing Warrior Series 88. London: Osprey Publishing Ltd., 2004.

McCulloch, Ian and Todish, Timothy J. *Through So Many Dangers: The Memoirs and Adventures of Robert Kirk, Late of the Royal Highland Regiment.* Fleischmanns, NY: Purple Mountain Press, Ltd., 2004.

Ness, Gary C. *Scoouwa: James Smith's Indian Captive Narrative.* Ohio: Ohio Historical Society, 1978.

Parkman, Francis. *Montcalm and Wolfe: The French and Indian War.* New York: De Capo Press, Inc., a Subsidiary of Plenum Publishing Corporation, 1995.

Peckham, Howard H. *The Colonial Wars, 1689-1762.* Chicago and London: The University of Chicago Press, 1964.

Penhallow, Samuel. *History of the Indian Wars.* Massachusetts: Corner House Publishers, 1973.

Philbrick, Nathaniel. *Mayflower.* London: Penguin Books, 2006

Rogers, Robert. *The Journals of Major Robert Rogers. Reprint of the 1769 Dublin edition. Published as Warfare on the Colonial American Frontier: The Journals of Major Robert Rogers & An Historical Account of the Expedition Against the Ohio Indians in the Year 1764, Under the Command of Henry Bouquet, Esq.* Bargersville, Indiana: Dresslar Publishing, 1997.

Rogers, Robert J. *Rising Above Circumstances: The Rogers Family in Colonial America.* Quebec, Canada: Sheltus & Picard Inc., 1998.

Schaaphok, Peter. *The Militia-Man.* London 1740. Schenectady: Reprinted by United States Historical Research Service 1995.

Speare, Elizabeth George. *Life In Colonial America.*. New York: Random House Inc. 1963.

Starbuck, David R. *The Great Warpath: British Military Sites from Albany to Crown Point.* Hanover, NH: University Press of New England, 1999.

Titus, Timothy D. *An Illustrated History of Crown Point.* New York: NYS Office of Parks, Recreation, and Historic Preservation, 1994.

Todish, Tim. *America's First First World War, The French and Indian War, 1754-1763.* Fleischmanns, New York: Purple Mountain Press, Second Edition. 2002

Todish, Tim and Harburn, Todd. *A Most Troublesome Situation, The British Military and the Pontiac Indian Uprising of 1763-1764.* Fleischmanns, New York: Purple Mountain Press LTD. 2006.

Todish, Timothy, and Zaboly, Gary. *The Annotated and Illustrated Journals of Major Robert Rogers.* Fleischmanns, New York: Purple Mountain Press LTD. 2002

Zaboly, Gary. *American Colonial Ranger, The Northern Colonies 1724-64.* Great Britain: Osprey Publishing Ltd. 2004

Zaboly, Gary. *A True Ranger, The Life and Many Wars of Major Robert Rogers.* New York: Royal Blockhouse LLC. 2004

Provincial Papers and Documents:
Documents and Records of the Province of New Hampshire from 1738 to 1749. Volume 5.

Documents and Records of the Province of New Hampshire from 1749 to 1763. Volume 6.

Index

Abenaki Indians, 65, 73, 119

Acadia, 13, 15, 20, 62, 90

Algonquin Indians, 13

Allegheny River, 18, 138, 140

ambush, 12, 37, 38, 40, 46, 47, 50, 54, 56, 74, 75, 78, 80, 81, 102, 108, 109, 111, 120, 124, 129, 130, 133, 140, 141, 142

Annapolis Royal, 101

Annawon, 47

Atlantic Ocean, 6

Awashonks,, 37

bateau, 100

Battle of Bloody Brook, 12

Battle of Lake George, 20, 21, 97

Battle of Sainte-Foy, 24

Battle on Snowshoes, 33, 103, 149

Benjamin Church, 7, 9, 13, 35, 36, 37, 41, 42, 44, 48, 55, 59, 63, 73, 75, 99, 147

blankets, 30, 74, 75, 76, 98, 110

Boston, 10, 38, 42, 48, 50, 52, 53, 55, 56, 58, 59, 63, 73, 74, 77, 89, 98, 100, 137, 151

breech-cloth, 30

Brookfield, 11, 42

canoes, 39, 52, 55, 58, 59, 69, 98, 108, 121, 141

Captain John Knox, 91

Captain John Rutherford, 29

Captain Josiah Standish, 13

Captain Pierre Pouchot, 23, 32

Captain Quinton Kennedy, 118

Captain Roger Goulding, 40

cartridge box, 31

Casco Harbor, 7, 49, 51, 53

Chief Paugus, 77, 78, 80

Christianity, 11

Church of England, 6

Colonel Daniel Brodhead, 138, 139, 140

Colonel John Bradstreet, 22

Colonel Joseph Blanchard, 96

Companie Franches de la Marine, 12

Connecticut, 12, 6, 13, 42, 95, 96, 115, 121, 122, 149

Crown Point, 24, 118, 119, 122, 131, 153

cutlass, 40

Dartmouth, 11

Deerfield, 7, 12, 14, 28, 42, 59, 63, 65, 66, 67, 68

Dummer's War, 15, 69, 70, 73, 81

Dunbarton, 95

Edmund Andros, 10

European military tactics, 11, 12, 27, 147

firelock, 31

Fort #4, 9

Fort Augusta, 9

Fort Beausejour, 5, 20, 90

Fort Bedford, 9, 128

Fort Carillon, 5, 21, 22, 24, 99, 101, 102, 109, 112, 113, 115, 116, 117

Fort Caroline, 1

Fort Chambly, 5

Fort Cumberland, 9, 90, 93

Fort de Chartres, 5

Fort Detroit, 5, 22, 25, 93, 123, 124, 128, 137

Fort Dummer, 9, 73

Fort Duquesne, 5, 18, 20, 21, 22, 25, 98, 129, 130

Fort Edward, 9, 21, 101, 103, 110, 111, 112, 113, 115, 116, 150

Fort Frontenac, 5, 22

Fort King George, 9

Fort Laurens, 138, 139

Fort Lawrence, 90

Fort Le Boeuf, 5, 17, 18

Fort Ligonier, 9, 128

Fort Loudoun, 9, 129

Fort Louis, 5

Fort Machault, 5

Fort McIntosh, 138, 139, 140

Fort Michilimackinac, 5, 123, 128

Fort Niagara, 5, 19, 22, 23

157

Fort Orange, 9, 14

Fort Oswego, 9

Fort Pitt, 25, 128, 138, 140

Fort Presque Isle, 5, 17, 128

Fort Prince George, 9

Fort Roselie, 5

Fort St. Frederic, 5, 20, 96, 97, 99, 101, 116, 117

Fort St. John, 5

Fort Stanwix, 9

Fort Toulouse, 5

Fort William Henry, 9, 21, 33, 97, 99, 100, 101, 102, 103

Fort Wm. Henry, 9

Fortress Louisbourg, 5, 16, 21

French and Indian War, 16, 19, 28, 32, 33, 89, 95, 96, 127, 134, 137, 147, 149, 150, 152, 153, 154

French Canadian partisan fighters, 27

fur trade, 2, 6, 7, 16, 18

Gary Zaboly, 9

General Anthony Wayne., 144

General Edward Braddock, 19, 98

General Josiah Harmar, 144

General James Abercrombie, 21

General William Haviland, 24

George Bray, 9

George Washington, 18, 21, 30

Gorham's Rangers, 91

Governor Arthur St. Clair, 144

Governor Simon Bradford, 37

Governor George Clinton, 17, 18

Governor James Delancey, 31

Governor Charles Longueuil, 17

Governor Robert Dinwiddie, 18

Grand Banks, 2

Great Lakes, 2, 3, 20, 127, 128, 130, 131

Great Swamp Fight, 12

Halifax, 9, 89, 103

Harvard, 11

hatchet, 11, 31, 41, 42, 43, 105

Hudson River, 21, 101

Hudson's Bay Company, 7

Ice skates, 33

Indian file, 75, 102

Iroquois, 2, 14, 17

Irregulars, 90, 100

Jacques Cartier, 1

James Smith, 11, 127, 128, 129, 130, 131, 133, 134, 135, 152

James Wolfe, 21, 22, 91

Jamestown Settlement, 6

Jeffery Amherst, 21, 22, 91, 116, 127

Jockey Caps, 30, 92

John Campbell, the Earl of Loudoun, 100

John Forbes, 21, 22

John Sassamon, 11

Joseph Coulon de Jumonville, 19

Josiah Winslow, 35, 42

Kennebeck River, 55, 69, 73

Kentucky, 15

King George's War, 15, 16, 70, 91, 95

King Louis XIV, 2

King Philip's War, 10, 11, 35, 47, 48

King William, 13, 14, 35, 48, 51, 53, 59, 64, 65

King William the 3rd, 13

King William's War, 13, 14, 35, 48, 51, 59, 64, 65

King's Rangers, 124

La Barbue Creek, 103

La Petite Guerre, 12

Lake Champlain, 9, 20, 21, 24, 96, 99, 101, 110, 115, 116, 117, 120, 122, 149, 151

Lake Ontario, 19, 20, 22, 24, 122

Lancaster, 11, 42

League of Augsburg, 13

linear formations, 23, 27

Logstown, 17

Lord Howe, 104, 112, 113

Lord Loudoun, 20, 21, 103, 104, 105, 110, 112

Lovewell's War, 15, 81

Maine, 6, 35, 42, 48, 49, 50, 51, 53, 56, 64, 73, 75

Major Cudworth, 37

Major George Scott, 91, 115

Massachusetts Bay, 12, 6, 37, 53, 59

Massasoit, 11

matchlock muskets, 41

Mendon, 11

Merrimack River, 74, 95

Metacom's War, 10

Middleborough, 11

Militia, 12, 18, 150, 153

Mississippi River, 3, 18

Mohegan,, 10

Monongahela River, 130

Narragansett Indians, 10, 11, 12, 13, 42

New England, 12, 10, 11, 12, 13, 14, 48, 59, 65, 66, 70, 71, 72, 73, 77, 90, 91, 96, 97, 116, 119, 121, 122, 150, 153

New Hampshire, 48, 51, 56, 59, 73, 95, 96, 154

New Orleans, 1, 3

New York., 9, 11, 99

Newfoundland, 1, 2, 6, 15, 16, 93

Northfield, 12

Nova Scotia, 4, 8, 14, 15, 20, 21, 57, 89, 90, 91, 92, 93, 96, 103, 104

Ohio, 9, 13, 3, 15, 16, 17, 18, 19, 20, 30, 127, 128, 129, 130, 138, 139, 143, 144, 145, 150, 152

Ohio River Valley, 3, 145, 150

Old Britain, 17

Ottawa, 2, 17, 25, 127, 128

Pequawket, 75, 77, 78, 81

Pequot, 10, 11, 12

Pickawillany Village, 17

Pierre de Rigaud Marquis de Vaudreuil, 65

Piscataqua River, 56

Plains of Abraham, 23, 92, 118

Plymouth Colony, 6, 11, 12, 13, 35, 37, 41, 47, 48

Pokanoket Indian village, 39

Pontiacs Rebellion, 11

Popham Colony, 6

Port Royal, 9, 14, 15, 61, 62, 63

Powder horns, 31

Proprietary Governors, 6

Providence, 10, 13, 35, 41

provisions, 29, 32, 41, 44, 48, 52, 54, 55, 56, 62, 63, 65, 68, 75, 98, 99, 115, 121, 122, 129, 139

Puritans, 6, 11

Quebec, 1, 2, 5, 14, 15, 21, 22, 24, 91, 92, 116, 118, 119, 122, 131, 151, 152

Queen Anne's War, 14, 35, 59, 69, 73

Queen Elizabeth the 1st, 6

Queen Mary, 53

Queen's Rangers, 124

Rangers, 9, 11, 13, 28, 31, 33, 35, 48, 63, 72, 73, 81, 89, 92, 93, 95, 99, 100, 101, 104, 105, 112, 115, 117, 118, 119, 120, 122, 124, 127, 128, 137, 139, 148, 150, 151

Rene' Robert Cavelier, Sieur de la Salle, 3

Revolutionary War, 11, 25, 124, 137, 143, 144

Rhode Island, 6, 12, 13, 35, 42, 47

rifles, 134

Rigaud de Vaudreuil, 24

Roanoke Colony, 6

Robert Monckton, 20, 90

Robert Rogers, 9, 11, 13, 28, 31, 95, 96, 98, 99, 104, 116, 119, 122, 123, 124, 147, 150, 152, 153, 154

Rogers' Rangers, 151

Roman Catholic Church, 16

round hats, 30

Saco Pond, 79, 81

Sakonnet Tribe, 35

Salem, 10

Sam Brady's Rangers, 11

Samuel de Champlain, 2

Saratoga, 15

scalping knife, 32

Scotch Bonnets, 30

Pierre-Joseph Celoron, 16

sentries, 46, 65

Seth Wyman, 69, 78, 79, 80

shot bags, 31, 49, 130

siege, 20, 21, 22, 23, 24, 25, 43, 90, 91, 103, 113, 115, 117, 118, 119, 122, 124, 128, 130, 139

Simon Bradstreet, 48

Sir William Phips, 53

sledges, 32

Smallpox, 10

snowshoe, 32, 68, 69, 70, 72

161

South Carolina, 1, 15, 123, 152

St. Augustine, 1, 14

St. Francis Raid, 119, 151

St. Johns River, 1

St. Lawrence River, 1, 2, 15, 21, 22, 91, 118, 122, 131

Stockbridge Indians, 110

Swansea, 11, 37, 38

Tanaghrisson, 19

temporary shelters, 29

The Marquis de Montcalm, 20

The Seven Years War, 16

Thomas Pray, 9

Ticonderoga, 21, 22, 23, 97, 99, 111, 113, 116, 122, 150, 154

Tim Green, 9

Tim Todish, 9

toboggans, 32, 33

Tom Shisler, 9, 34

Treaty of Aix-la-Chapelle, 16

Treaty of Greenville, 145

Treaty of Paris, 25, 127, 143

Treaty of Ryswick, 14

Treaty of Utrecht, 15

Trois Rivieres, 5

United States Army Rangers, 13, 33

Virginia, 11, 12, 6, 18, 19, 69, 137, 139, 150, 152

Virginia Company of London, 6

volleys of musket fire, 23, 41

Wabash River, 144

Wampanoag Indians, 10, 11, 37

Wamsutta, 11

war of attrition, 98

War of Austrian Succession, 15

whaleboat, 123

William Johnson, 17, 20, 21, 23, 97, 100, 150

Windsor, 10

woodland skills, 28

About the Author

Matt Wulff is a self described mechanic by day and an amateur Author/Historian by night. Matt's lifelong love of colonial history, plus he and his wife Beth's participation in Living History events specific to the French and Indian War, has led him to doing historical research of the time period.

Matt's research efforts led him to try his hand at writing about some of his discoveries. He has had articles published in Smoke and Fire News, The Battalion Journal, Muzzleloader Magazine, and On the Trail Magazine. Matt also had his first book, Robert Rogers Rules for the Ranging Service, An Analysis, published in April of 2006.

The picture above is of Matt and Beth while attending the Grand Encampment of the French and Indian War at Fort Ticonderoga in 2007.

www.ingramcontent.com/pod-product-compliance
Lightning Source LLC
Chambersburg PA
CBHW050814160426
43192CB00010B/1760